CW01455520

# Preface

The European Computer Driving Licence (ECDL) is an internationally recognized qualification in end-user computer skills. It is designed to give employers and job-seekers a standard against which they can measure competence – not in theory, but in practice. Its seven Modules cover the areas most frequently required in today's business environment. More than one million people in over fifty countries have undertaken ECDL in order to benefit from the personal, social and business advantages and international mobility that it provides.

In addition to its application in business, the ECDL has a social and cultural purpose. With the proliferation of computers into every aspect of modern life, there is a danger that society will break down into two groups – the information 'haves' and the information 'have nots'. The seven modules of the ECDL are not difficult, but they equip anyone who passes them to participate actively and fully in the Information Society.

The ECDL is not product-specific – you can use any hardware or software to perform the tasks in the examinations. And you can take the seven examinations in any order, and work through the syllabus at your own pace.

This book is one of a set of seven, each dealing with one of the ECDL modules. While each book can be used independently, if you are new to computers, you should read Module 2, *Using a Computer and managing files*, before attempting any of the other practical modules (such as this one). Module 2 teaches you the basic operations that are needed in the other practical modules.

The examples in these books are based on PCs (rather than Apple Macintoshes), and on Microsoft software, as follows:

- Operating system: Microsoft Windows 95/98
- Word Processing: Microsoft Word 2000
- Spreadsheets: Microsoft Excel 2000
- Databases: Microsoft Access 2000
- Presentations: Microsoft PowerPoint 2000
- Information and Communication: Microsoft Internet Explorer 5.0 and Microsoft Outlook Express 5.0

If you use other hardware or software, you can use the principles discussed in this book, but the details of operation will differ.

Welcome to the world of computers!

# ECDL3

module 3

**for Microsoft Office 2000**

## Word processing

# ECDL3

## for Microsoft Office 2000

**Brendan Munnelly and Paul Holden**

# Word processing

*Everything you need to pass the European
Computer Driving Licence®, module by module*

Prentice
Hall

*An imprint of* **Pearson Education**

London · New York · Sydney · Tokyo · Singapore ·
Madrid · Mexico City · Munich · Paris

PEARSON EDUCATION LIMITED

Head Office:
Edinburgh Gate
Harlow CM20 2JE
Tel: +44 (0)1279 623623
Fax: +44 (0)1279 431059

London Office:
128 Long Acre
London WC2E 9AN
Tel: +44 (0)20 7447 2000
Fax: +44 (0)20 7240 5771

Website: www.it-minds.com

This edition published in Great Britain in 2002
First published in Great Britain in 2002 as part of
*ECDL3 The Complete Coursebook for Microsoft Office 2000*

© Rédacteurs Limited 2002

ISBN 0-130-35450-3

*British Library Cataloguing in Publication Data*
A CIP catalogue record for this book can be obtained from the British Library

All rights reserved; no part of this publication may be reproduced, stored in a retrieval system, or transmitted in any form or by any means, electronic, mechanical, photocopying, recording, or otherwise without either the prior written permission of the Publishers or a license permitting restricted copying in the United Kingdom issued by the Copyright Licensing Agency Ltd, 90 Tottenham Court Road, London W1P 0LP. This book may not be lent, resold, hired out or otherwise disposed of by way of trade in any form of binding or cover other than that in which it is published, without the prior consent of the Publishers.

'European Computer Driving Licence' and ECDL and Stars device are registered trademarks of the European Computer Driving Licence Foundation Limited. Rédacteurs Limited is an independent entity from the European Computer Driving Licence Foundation Limited, and not affiliated with the European Computer Driving Licence Foundation in any manner.

This book may be used in assisting students to prepare for the European Computer Driving Licence examination. Neither the European Computer Driving Licence Foundation Limited, Rédacteurs Limited nor the publisher warrants that the use of this book will ensure passing the relevant examination.

Use of the ECDL-F approved Courseware logo on this product signifies that it has been independently reviewed and approved in complying with the following standards:

Acceptable coverage of all courseware content related to ECDL syllabus Module 3 version 3.0. This courseware material has not been reviewed for technical accuracy and does not guarantee that the end user will pass the associated ECDL examinations. Any and all assessment tests and/or performance based exercises contained in these Modular books relate solely to these books and do not constitute, or imply, certification by the European Driving Licence Foundation in respect of any ECDL examinations. For details on sitting ECDL examinations in your country please contact the local ECDL licensee or visit the European Computer Driving Licence Foundation Limited web site at http://www.ecdl.com.

References to the European Computer Driving Licence (ECDL) include the International Computer Driving Licence (ICDL).

ECDL Foundation Syllabus Version 3.0 is published as the official syllabus for use within the European Computer Driving Licence (ECDL) and International Computer Driving Licence (ICDL) certification programmes.

Rédacteurs Limited is at http://www.redact.ie

Brendan Munnelly is at http://www.munnelly.com

10 9 8 7 6 5 4 3 2 1

Typeset by Pantek Arts, Maidstone, Kent.
Printed and bound in Great Britain by Ashford Colour Press, Gosport, Hampshire.

*The Publishers' policy is to use paper manufactured from sustainable forests.*

# CONTENTS

CHAPTER 5

# Mail merge and templates   125

# Introduction

**B**ack in the days when people thought they could predict the future, someone came up with the phrase 'paperless office'.

As computers found their way into more and more workplaces, the theory was that paper-based communication would disappear. Forever.

But alongside affordable computers came affordable printers. As a result, computerization has led to more rather than less paper usage. The office-supplies people have never been busier.

In this word processing module, you will learn how to add further to the world's output of computer-generated paperwork.

You will discover how to create formal business letters and reports, and produce stylish posters and restaurant menus. We will even share with you the secrets of generating personalized form letters, (un)popularly known as junk mail.

Good luck with it.

# CHAPTER 1

# Your first letter in Word

## In this chapter

There is a lot more to word processing than just typing and editing words, but these are the two basics. Read the material and follow the examples in this chapter and you will have the foundation skills to move on to more advanced tasks.

You will also learn how to access and search through Word's online help, which is a great place to find answers and advice on using any of the program's features.

### New skills

At the end of this chapter you should be able to:
- Start and quit Word
- Enter and edit text

- Recognize Word's non-printing characters
- Use the Shift, Backspace, Delete, arrow, and Tab keys
- Type and print a standard letter
- Use Word's Insert Date feature
- Reverse typing and editing actions with Word's Undo feature
- Save, name, open, create, and close Word documents
- Use online help to learn more about Word

**New words**

At the end of this chapter you should be able to explain the following terms:
- Document
- Paragraph mark
- Wrap around
- Non-printing characters

# Starting Word

**D**ouble-click on the Microsoft Word icon or choose **Start | Programs | Microsoft Word**. Word starts and displays a new window containing a new, blank document ready for you to type into.

Word 2000

*A blank Word document ready to accept your text*

### Word document

*A Microsoft Word file, for example, a letter or a report.*

## What? No new, blank document?

If starting Word did not automatically open a new, blank document, click on the New button at the top-left of your screen.

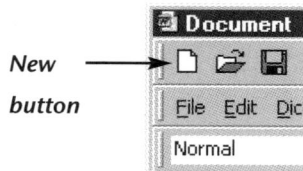

*New button*

# Text cursor and paragraph mark

Near the top-left corner of your document you can see two items:

- **Text cursor**: A blinking vertical line. Whenever you type text, Word places the text at the text cursor's location. Think of the cursor as a 'you are here' indicator, telling you where you are in a document.

- **Paragraph mark**: Every new Word document contains one of these (it looks like a backwards letter P). Whenever you press the Enter key to begin a new paragraph, Word inserts another one at that point. The paragraph mark appears on the screen only and not on printouts.

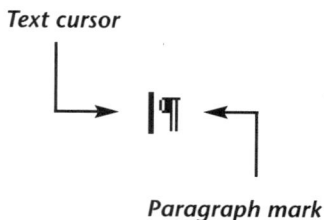

*Text cursor*

*Paragraph mark*

### Paragraph mark

*A symbol shown on the screen (but not printed) to indicate the end of a paragraph. Word displays one each time that you press the Enter key.*

### What? No paragraph mark?

If Word does not display the paragraph mark in your document, click on the Show/Hide Paragraph Mark button at the top of the screen, near the top-right corner of your Word window.

*Show/Hide Paragraph*
*Mark button*

# Actions you need to know

Here are the four basic operations in Word that you need to know:

- Typing text

- Editing (changing) text you previously typed

- Using the Shift key to type upper-case (capital) letters

- Using the Enter key to type new paragraph marks

You will practise each one in the following four exercises.

### Exercise 1.1: Typing text in Word

1  Type the following number: 7

2  Press the spacebar. Word displays a dot on the screen. This is Word's way of telling that you have typed a space. Word will not print the dot.

7·dwarfs

3  Type the following six letters: dwarfs

That's it. Congratulations! You have typed your first text in Word.

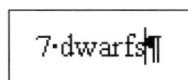

## Exercise 1.2: Editing previously typed text

Often you will want to change – or, perhaps, remove completely – text that you have typed. This is called editing.

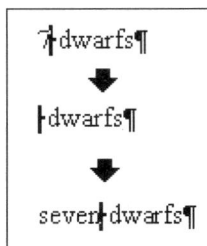

1  Using the mouse, click to the right of the 7.

2  Press the Backspace key. (You will find it directly above the Enter key.)

3  Type the following word: seven

You have completed the editing exercise.

## Exercise 1.3: Using the Shift key

1  Click to the left of the letter s in seven.

2  Press the Delete key to delete the letter s.

3  Hold down the Shift key and type the letter s. Word displays an upper-case S.

4  Move the cursor to the right of the letter d in dwarfs.

5  Press the Backspace key to delete the letter d.

6  Hold down the Shift key and type the letter d. Word displays an upper-case D.

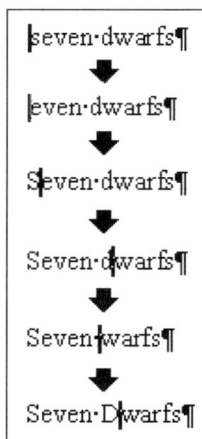

Well done! Another exercise completed.

### Exercise 1.4: Using Enter to type new paragraph marks

1  Now you will use the Enter key to end one paragraph and begin another.

2  Click to the right of the word Dwarfs, and press Enter. This creates a new paragraph. Word places the cursor at the start of a new line.

3  Type: John

4  Press Enter.

5  Type: Paul

6  Press Enter.

7  Type George

8  Press Enter.

9  Type Ringo.

John¶
Paul¶
George¶
Ringo¶

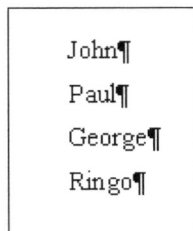

You will not need this text for future exercises. So delete it as follows:

10  Click to the right of the word Ringo.

11  Press and hold down the Backspace key until Word has removed all the text from the document.

# Keys you need to know

Now is a good time to summarize the role of these important keys:

- **Shift**: Pressed in combination with a letter, this creates an upper-case letter. Pressed in combination with a number or symbol key,

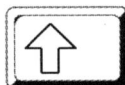

it creates the upper symbol. You will find a Shift key at both sides of the keyboard.

- **Backspace**: Deletes the character to the *left* of the cursor. You will find the Backspace key at the top-right of the keyboard, just above the Enter key.

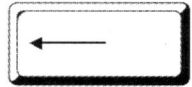

- **Delete**: Deletes the character to the *right* of the cursor. You will find the Delete key in a group of six keys to the right of the Enter key.

- **Arrows**: Rather than use the mouse to move the cursor around your document, you can press any of the four arrow keys, located to the right of the Enter key. You may find this method faster than moving and clicking the mouse, because you need not take either hand away from the keyboard.

# Typing a letter

Now you are ready to type a longer piece of text, a letter.

### Exercise 1.5: Typing a paragraph of a letter

1   Type the following text:

I am writing to you in relation to our annual Sale of Work which will take place in our local Scout Hall on 17 October next.

Your screen should look as follows:

> ⌶·am·writing·to·you·in·relation·to·our·annual·Sale·of·Work·which·will·take·place·in·our·local·
> Scout·Hall·on·17·October·next.¶

Notice how Word moved the cursor to the beginning of the next line when the text you were typing reached the right-hand edge of the page.

On an old-style typewriter, you would have needed to press the Enter (also called return) key to move down to the next line. Word does this for you automatically. This feature is called wrap-around, and Word is said to 'wrap' the text to a new line once the previous line is full.

### Wrap-around

> *Word's automatic moving of the cursor to the beginning of a new line when the text reaches the end of the previous one.*

### Exercise 1.6: Typing more text in your letter

In this exercise, you will type more text in the letter, and type your name at the bottom.

*Click here*

↓

I·am·writing·to

1  Click at the beginning of the first line, so that the cursor is just to the left of the letter 'I'.

2  Press the Enter key to create a new paragraph, and then the 'up' arrow key to position the cursor at the start of the new paragraph.

3  Type the following and press Enter:

Dear Ms Smith

Your letter should look as shown.

---

Dear·Ms·Smith¶

I·am·writing·to·you·in·relation·to·our·annual·Sale·of·Work·which·will·take·place·in·our·local·
Scout·Hall·on·17·October·next.¶

---

**4** Click at the end of the last line, so that the cursor is just to the right of the full stop and to the left of the paragraph mark.

---

|I·am·writing·to·you·in·relation·to·our·annual·Sale·of·Work·which·will·take·place·in·our·local·
Scout·Hall·on·17·October·next.¶

---

*Click here*

**5** Press Enter twice.

**6** Type the following and press Enter twice:

In previous years your company was kind enough to donate a prize for our wheel of fortune.

**7** Type the following and press Enter twice:

Could we ask you to be as generous again this year?

**8** Type the following:

Ken Bloggs

Your letter should look as shown.

---

Dear·Ms·Smith¶

I·am·writing·to·you·in·relation·to·our·annual·Sale·of·Work·which·will·take·place·in·our·local·
Scout·Hall·on·17·October.¶

¶

In·previous·years·your·company·was·kind·enough·to·donate·a·prize·for·our·wheel·of·fortune.¶

¶

Could·we·ask·you·to·be·as·generous·again?¶

¶

Ken·Bloggs¶

**9**   Click at the beginning of the sender's name, so that the cursor is just to the left of the letter 'K' in 'Ken'. Press Enter to create a new line.

**10**   Hold down the Shift key and press the hyphen key about twenty times. (The hyphen key is the second key to the left of the Backspace key.)

_____¶

Ken·Bloggs¶

The Hyphen key (left
of the Equals key)

Release the Shift key.

When you print the letter, you can write your signature on the line created by the repeated pressing of the hyphen.

That's it. You have completed the exercise.

No letter is complete with an address and a date. In Exercises 1.7 and 1.8 you will discover how you can use Word's Tab key to position an address, and the **Date and Time** command on the **Insert** menu to insert today's date in a letter or other document.

## Exercise 1.7: Entering an address on a letter

**1**   Click at the beginning of the line containing 'Dear Ms Smith', so that the cursor is just to the left of the letter 'D'.

**2**   Press Enter seven times to create new lines at the top of your letter. This is where you will type the address and, in Exercise 1.8, the date.

**3**   Click at the beginning of the first line, so that the cursor is at the top-left of your letter.

4    Press the Tab key eight times, and type
the following:

24 Main Street

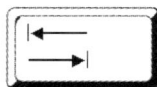

*Tab key*

5    Click at the beginning of the second line,
press the Tab key eight times, and type the following:

Anytown

6    Click at the beginning of the third line, press the Tab key
eight times, and type the following:

333444

The top of your letter should now look as shown.

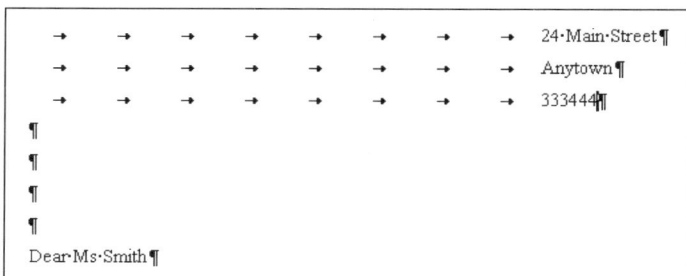

## Exercise 1.8: Entering a date on a letter

1    Click at the beginning of the line containing 'Dear Ms
Smith', so that the cursor is just to the left of the letter 'D'.

2    Press the 'up' arrow key three times, and then press the
Tab key eight times. You are now ready to insert a date
on the letter.

3    Choose **Insert | Date and Time**.

Word displays a dialog box that shows today's date in a
variety of formats.

**4** Select the date format you want, and click **OK**.

This inserts the date in your letter, and closes the dialog box.

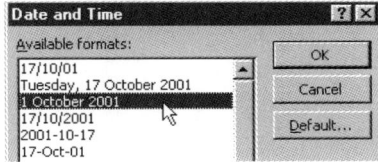

**Date and Time**

Available formats:

17/10/01
Tuesday, 17 October 2001
1 October 2001
17/10/2001
2001-10-17
17-Oct-01

OK
Cancel
Default...

Well done. The heading of your first letter in Word should look as follows.

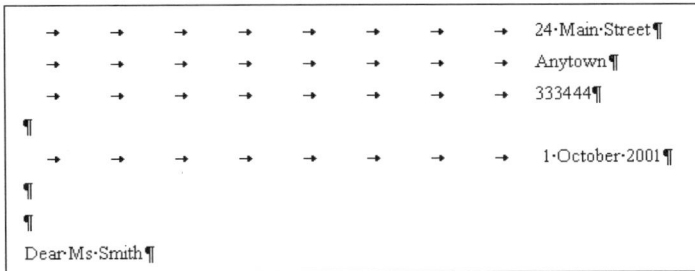

```
 →       →       →       →       →       →       →       →    24·Main·Street¶
 →       →       →       →       →       →       →       →    Anytown¶
 →       →       →       →       →       →       →       →    333444¶
¶
 →       →       →       →       →       →       →       →    1·October·2001¶
¶
¶
Dear·Ms·Smith¶
```

## Non-printing characters and wavy underlines

Each time you press the Tab key, Word inserts an arrow symbol on the screen. Like the paragraph mark that indicates a paragraph ending, and the dot between words that represents a blank space, the tab symbol is a non-printing character.

### Non-printing characters
*Symbols that Word displays on the screen to help you type and edit your document, but that are not printed.*

Depending on how Word is set up on your computer, you may see green and/or red wavy underlines beneath certain words or phrases. These have

Ken·Bloggs¶

*Wavy underlines indicate possible spelling or grammar problem*

to do with Word's spell- and grammar-checking features, which are explained in Chapter 3. Until then, ignore them.

# Printing your letter

Your letter is ready to be printed out. Choose **File | Print**. If your printer is set up correctly all you need to do is click **OK** on the Print dialog box. You will learn more about printing in Chapter 3.

# Word's toolbars

Word's toolbars give you convenient, one-click access to the commands that you use most often. By default, Word displays two toolbars, the Standard and Formatting toolbars, on a *single* row across the top of the screen.

To display them as two, individual toolbars, follow these steps:

- Choose **Tools | Customize** and click the **Options** tab.

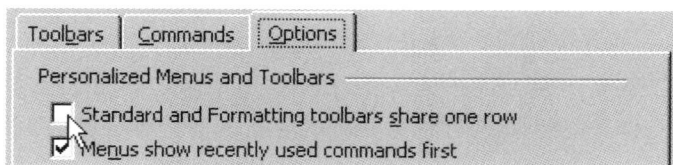

- Deselect the Standard and Formatting toolbars share one row checkbox, and click **Close**.

### Hiding and displaying toolbars

You can display or hide Word's various toolbars by choosing the **View | Toolbars** command, and then selecting or deselecting the various toolbar options from the drop-down menu displayed.

*The check marks beside the Standard, Formatting, and Drawing toolbars indicate that they are already selected for display on screen.*

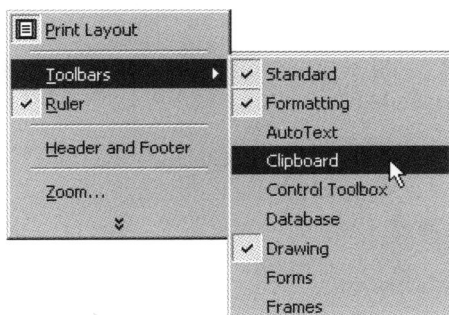

# The Standard and Formatting toolbars

Only two of Word's toolbars are relevant to this ECDL module: the Standard toolbar and the Formatting toolbar.

*Word's Standard toolbar*

The Standard toolbar includes buttons for managing files – that is, Word documents – and for working with tables.

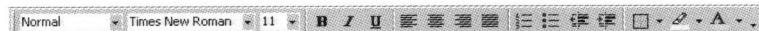

*Word's Formatting toolbar*

The Formatting toolbar includes buttons for changing the appearance of text, and for inserting bullets.

Rather than introduce all these buttons at once, we will explain the ones you need to know about as they become relevant through the remainder of this ECDL Word Processing module.

## Hiding and displaying toolbar buttons

You can remove one or more buttons from a toolbar. Follow these steps:

- Display the toolbar that you want to change.

- Hold down the Alt key, and drag the button off the toolbar.

Word removes the selected button from the toolbar. Want the button back again? Follow this procedure:

- Display the toolbar. Click on **More Buttons** (at the very end of the toolbar) and then on **Add or Remove Buttons**.

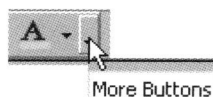

- Click the button you want to display again.

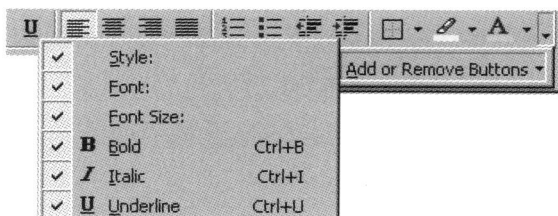

- Click anywhere outside the menu to close it.

Word redisplays the button on the toolbar.

# Word's personalized menus

By default, when you first choose a
menu, Word displays only *some* of
the commands on that menu. To
view a complete list, click the double-
arrow at the bottom of the menu.

If you choose a command that is
not displayed by default, Word adds
it to the displayed list the next time
you choose the menu.

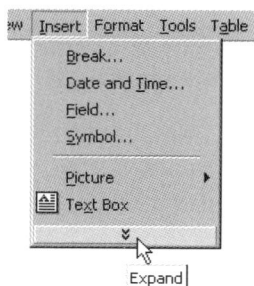

To view *all* commands each time you choose a menu, follow
these steps:

* Choose **Tools | Customize** and click the **Options** tab.

* Deselect the Menus show recently used commands first
  option, and click **Close**.

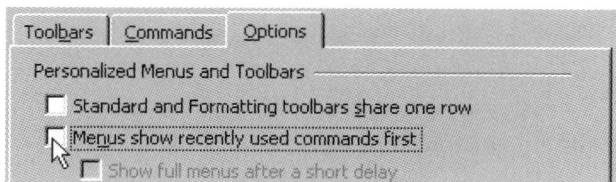

# Word's Undo feature

Did you enter the wrong text? Press the wrong key? Word's
Undo feature enables you to reverse your most recent typing
or editing action if it has produced
unwanted results:

* Choose **Edit | Undo** or click the Undo
  button on the Standard toolbar.

Pressing Undo repeatedly reverses your last series of actions. To view a list of recent actions that you can undo, click the arrow at the right of the Undo button. If you undo an action and then change your mind, click the Redo button (to the right of the Undo button).

# Online help

Like Excel, Access, PowerPoint, and other Microsoft applications, Word offers a searchable online help system.

- The word 'help' means that the information is there to help you understand and use the application.

- The word 'online' means that the material is presented on the computer screen rather than as a traditional printed manual.

You can search through and read online help in two ways: from the Help menu, or from dialog boxes.

## Using Help menu options

Choose **Help | Microsoft Word Help** or click the Online Help button on the Standard toolbar to display the three tabs of the Help Topics dialog box. These are explained on the following page.

As you search through and read online help topics, you will see the following buttons at the top of the online help window:

- **Hide/Show**: Hides or displays the left pane of the online help dialog box.

- **Back/Forward**: Moves you backwards and forwards through previously visited help topics.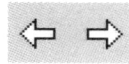

- **Print**: Prints the currently displayed help topic.

- **Options**: Offers a number of display choices.

| **Contents tab** | **Answer Wizard tab** | **Index tab** |
|---|---|---|
| This offers descriptions of Word's main features. | Type your question in the box at the top-left of the dialog box, and click **Search**. | Type the word or phrase you are interested in and click **Search**. |
| Where you see a heading with a book symbol, double-click it to view the related sub-headings. | Word displays all matches from the online help in the lower-left of the dialog box. | Word displays a list of suggested help topics in the lower-left of the dialog box. When you find the index entry that you are looking for, click it to display the associated text in the right pane. |
| Double-click on a question-mark symbol to read the online help text. | Click a topic to display the associated text in the right pane. | |

Take a few minutes to look through Word's online help system. Remember that you are free to use online help during an ECDL test.

## Using help from dialog boxes

You can also access online help directly from a dialog box, as Exercise 1.9 demonstrates.

## Exercise 1.9: Using online help in a dialog box

1 Choose **Edit | Find** to display the Find and Replace dialog box.

2 Click on the question-mark symbol near the top-right of the dialog box. Word displays a question mark to the right of the cursor.

3 Move the mouse down and right, and click anywhere in the Find what: box.

Word displays help text telling you about the Find what: box.

> Type the information you want to search for, paste it from the Clipboard, or click a recent entry from the list. To search for text that's in a particular format, click **Format**. If Word can't find the text you're searching for in your document, formatting search criteria may still be set from a previous search; if this is the case, click **No Formatting** to clear the formatting search criteria.

4 Click anywhere else on the Word window to remove the online help text, and then click **Cancel** to close the dialog box.

Practise this exercise with other dialog boxes in Word.

# Working with Word documents

A Word document is a file containing text (and sometimes graphics too).

## Saving your document

In Word, as in other applications, always save your work as you go along. Don't wait until you are finished! To save a document:

- Choose **File | Save** or click the Save button on the Standard toolbar.

*Save button*

The first time that you save a file in Word you are asked to specify:

- The location on your PC where you want your file saved.

- The name of your new file.

Exercise 1.10 leads you through the steps.

## Word file name extension

The file names of Word documents end in .doc. This helps you to distinguish Word files from other file types, such as Excel (.xls) or PowerPoint (.ppt) files.

## Exercise 1.10: Saving and naming a new document

1 Choose **File | Save** or click the Save button on the Standard toolbar.

2   The first time that you save a document, Word prompts
    you to select a location. By default, Word suggests that
    you save your files in the My Documents folder. Accept
    or amend this location, as required.

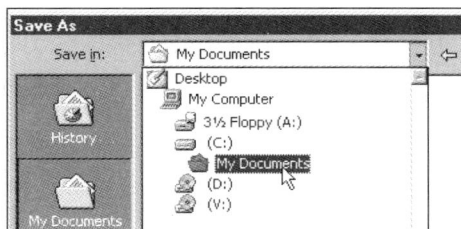

3   Word prompts you to give a name to your new file. Type a
    name that you will find easy to remember and recognize. If
    your initials are KB, for example, call it KBletter.

    You need not type '.doc' after your file name when
    saving a file. Word adds the three-letter file name
    extension automatically.

## Creating a new document

To create a new Word file:

*   Choose **File | New**.

    –or–

    Click the New button on the Standard toolbar.

*New button*

### Opening an existing document

To open an existing Word file:

Choose **File | Open**. Alternatively, click the
Open button on the Standard toolbar. Select
the file you want from the dialog box.

*Open button*

You can have multiple Word documents open at the
same time.

### Closing a document

To close a Word document:

*Close Word*

*Close document*

*   Choose **File | Close** or click
    the Close button on the
    document window.

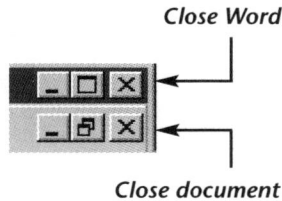

If you have made changes to your document since you last
saved it, Word prompts you to save the changes before it
closes the file.

# Quitting Word

To leave Word:

*   Choose **File | Exit** or click the Close button on the
    Word window.

If you have left open any files containing unsaved work,
Word prompts you to save them.

Well done. You have now completed Chapter 1 of the
ECDL *Word Processing* module.

# Chapter summary: so now you know

A Word *document* is a file containing text (and sometimes graphics too). Every new Word document contains a *text cursor*. Whenever you type text, Word places the text at the text cursor's location. You can move the text cursor with the mouse or with the arrow keys.

Every new document also contains a *paragraph mark*. Whenever you press the Enter key to type a new paragraph of text or insert a blank line, Word inserts another paragraph mark at that point.

You can edit text with the following two keys:

- **Backspace**: Removes text to the *left* of the text cursor

- **Delete**: Removes text to the *right* of the text cursor

Press the Shift key in combination with a letter, number, or symbol key to type an *upper-case* (capital) character or symbol.

Press the Tab key repeatedly to move text to the right. When typing a letter, for example, use Tab to position the address and related details at the top-right of the letter.

Word's *Insert Date* feature inserts the current date in a document. You can choose from a wide range of date formats.

Word's *non-printing characters*, such as a single dot to represent a space, do not appear on printouts. They are displayed on the screen only as a guide to typing and editing.

Word's *Undo* feature enables you to reverse your most recent typing or editing actions if they have produced unwanted results.

In Word, as in other applications, always save your work as you go along. The first time you save a document file, Word prompts you to give it a *file name*. Word automatically adds the file name extension *.doc* to all saved documents.

Word offers a searchable *online help* system that you can access in two ways: from the Help menu, and from the question-mark button at the top-right of individual dialog boxes.

# CHAPTER 2

# Formatting, positioning and copying text

## In this chapter

In addition to typing and editing text, you can use a word processor to:

• Change the *appearance* of the text. This is called formatting. It includes such actions as making text bolder (heavier), placing a line under it, and putting it in italics. You can also change the text font and font size, format text as bullets, and apply shading (coloured backgrounds) and borders to text.

• Change the *position* of text on the page. You have already learnt how to reposition text using the Tab key. Now you will discover two other methods: alignment and indenting.

In this chapter you will also learn how to copy text within and between documents, and how to insert symbols and special characters.

## New skills

At the end of this chapter you should be able to:

- Select text
- Format text (bold, italic and underline)
- Copy, cut, and paste text
- Indent text from the left and right page margins
- Align text (left, right, centre, and justified)
- Create text bullets
- Explain fonts and font sizes, and super- and subscripts
- Add borders and shading to text
- Use Word's Zoom feature to enlarge and reduce the document display
- Save a Word document to a diskette
- Insert symbols and special characters
- Use Word's Format Painter feature to copy formatting


## New words

At the end of this chapter you should be able to explain the following terms:

- Select
- Bulleted text
- Clipboard
- Font
- Indent

- Superscript
- Subscript
- Alignment
- Format Painter

# Selecting text

Typically, when you want to format or position some text, it is only a particular character, word, group of words or paragraph that you want to change.

You tell Word which part of the document you want to change by first selecting that text. Selecting a piece of text is sometimes called highlighting that text.

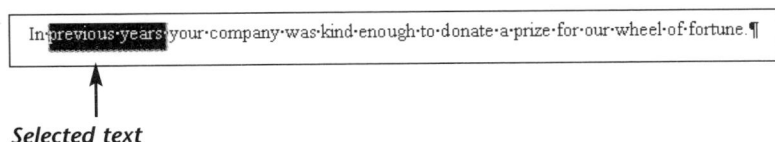

In previous years your·company·was·kind·enough·to·donate·a·prize·for·our·wheel·of·fortune.¶

*Selected text*

When you select text, Word displays that text in reverse (white text on black background), rather like the negative of a photograph.

### Selecting text

*Highlighting a piece of text in order to perform an action on it such as formatting or alignment.*

Formatting and alignment are just two of the actions that you will learn how to perform on selected text. In later chapters, you will learn how to find and replace, and spellcheck, selected text.

To select text within a Word document, first position the cursor at the beginning of the text that you want to select:

- To select text on a single line, drag the mouse to the right until you have selected the characters or words.

- To select a sentence or other piece of text that is on more than a single line, drag the mouse to the right and down the page.

**Ctrl**

*Ctrl (Control) key*

- To select your whole document, hold down the Ctrl key and click anywhere in the left margin.

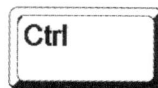

## Exercise 2.1: Selecting text

In this exercise you will learn how to select text – characters, words sentences and paragraphs.

1  Open Word, and open the letter you saved in Exercise 1.9 of Chapter 1.

2  Position the cursor to the left of the letter D in Dear Ms Smith.

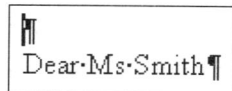

Dear·Ms·Smith¶

3  Drag the mouse to the right until you have selected the letter D. Release the mouse button.

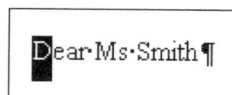

Dear·Ms·Smith¶

You have learned how to select a single character. Now click anywhere on the page to deselect the letter D. Deselecting a piece of text does not remove the text; it just means that it is no longer selected.

4  Again, position the mouse to the left of the letter D, but this time keep dragging with the mouse until you have selected the entire word Dear.

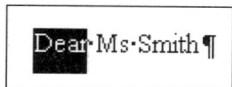

Dear·Ms·Smith¶

Release the mouse button.

5   Finally, position the mouse to the left of the letter D.
Now drag the mouse down and right until you have
selected the first paragraph of the letter.

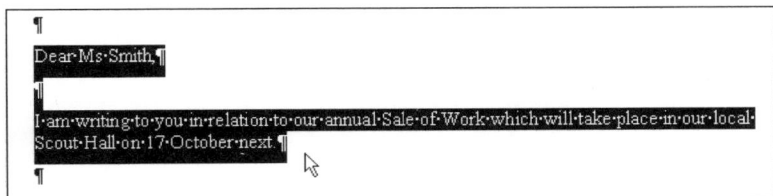

¶

Dear·Ms·Smith,¶

¶

I·am·writing·to·you·in·relation·to·our·annual·Sale·of·Work·which·will·take·place·in·our·local·
Scout·Hall·on·17·October·next.¶

¶

You have learned how to select several lines of text.
Click anywhere outside the selected area to deselect it.

That completes the exercise. But practise your text-selection
skills by clicking at any point in your document, and
dragging the mouse in various directions.

# Formatting text

Word's most commonly used formatting features are:

- **Bold**: Heavy black text, often used for headings

- *Italic*: Slanted text, often used for emphasis or
foreign words

- Underline: A single line under the text,
often used in legal documents and
beneath signatures on letters

**B**  *I*  <u>U</u>

*Format buttons*

You will find the relevant buttons on the Formatting toolbar.
In the next exercises you will learn how to apply the bold
and italic formats.

## Exercise 2.2: Applying the bold format

1   Place the cursor at the start of the first line of the address.

2   Drag right and down with the mouse until you have selected the two address lines and the phone number.

3   Click the Bold button or press CTRL+b (hold down CTRL and type b).

4   Deselect the lines by clicking on any other area of the document.

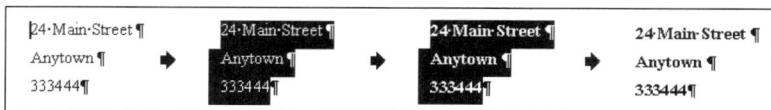

*Applying the bold format*

## Exercise 2.3: Applying the italic format

1   Place the cursor at the start of the name, Ken Bloggs.

2   Drag right until you have selected the name.

3   Click the Italic button or press Ctrl+i.

4   Deselect the name by clicking on any other area of the document.

Well done. Save your letter.

# Copying and pasting text

Suppose you want to use the same text – words or paragraphs – more than once in a document. Do you need to retype it each time that you need it? No.

With Word, you can type the text just once, and then insert it as many times as you need. This is a two-step process:

- **Copy:** You select and then *copy* the text to the clipboard, a temporary holding area.

- **Paste:** You insert or *paste* the text from the clipboard into a different part of the same document, or even a different document.

### Clipboard

*A temporary storage area to which you can copy text (or graphics). You can paste to any location within the same or different documents.*

## Exercise 2.4: Copying and pasting text within a document

1   Select the second paragraph of your letter.

> In·previous·years·your·company·was·kind·enough·to·donate·a·prize·for·our·wheel·of·fortune.¶

2   Click the Copy button on the Standard toolbar, or choose **Edit | Copy**.

*Copy button*

3   Position the cursor at the left of the paragraph mark on the next line.

> In·previous·years·your·company·was·kind·enough·to·donate·a·prize·for·our·wheel·of·fortune.¶
> ¶

4   Click the Paste button on the Standard toolbar, or choose **Edit | Paste**.

*Paste button*

In·previous·years·your·company·was·kind·enough·to·donate·a·prize·for·our·wheel·of·fortune.¶
In·previous·years·your·company·was·kind·enough·to·donate·a·prize·for·our·wheel·of·fortune.¶

**5** Select the line that you have pasted from the clipboard, and press the Delete key. You will not need it again.

## About the clipboard

Seven points that you should remember about the Word clipboard:

- The clipboard is temporary. Turn off your computer and the clipboard contents are deleted.

- The same clipboard is available to all Windows applications. For example, you can copy from Excel and paste into Word.

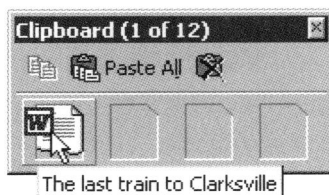

- The clipboard can hold up to *twelve* copied items at a time. When you copy the second and subsequent items, Word displays the Clipboard toolbar. (If it doesn't appear, choose **View** | **Toolbars** | **Clipboard** to display it.)

- Each copied item is added to the clipboard, and stored in the next available space. What happens if you attempt to copy a thirteenth item? Word responds by asking if you want to overwrite the oldest of the twelve items currently in the clipboard.

- If you rest the cursor over an item's icon on the clipboard toolbar, Word displays its first fifty characters (if the item is text) or a descriptive label (if it is a picture).

- To paste the most recently copied item from the clipboard, click the Paste button on the Standard toolbar, or choose **Edit | Paste**. To paste a different item, click its icon on the Clipboard toolbar. To paste all previously copied items (Word calls this 'Collect and Paste'), click the Paste All button on the Clipboard toolbar.

- An item stays in the clipboard after you paste from it, so you can paste the same piece of text into as many locations as you need.

## Exercise 2.5: Copying and pasting text between documents

The line you copied in Exercise 2.4 is still in the clipboard. In this exercise you will copy it to a different document.

*New button*

1 Click the New button to create a new, blank Word document.

Word places the cursor at the beginning of the document.

2 Click the Paste button on the Standard toolbar, or choose **Edit | Paste**.

3 Choose **File | Close** to close the new document. When Word asks you whether you want to save the new file, click **No**.

When you have more than one Word document open at a time, you can switch between them by choosing **Window | <document name>**.

### Cutting and pasting text

Sometimes, you may want to remove text from one
part of a document and place it in a different part.

Rather than deleting the text and then retyping it
elsewhere, Word allows you to move the text by
cutting it from its current location and pasting it to
the new location.

*Cut
button*

Cut-and-paste differs from copy-and-paste in that Word
removes the cut text, whereas copied text remains in its
original location. You can cut selected text by using the Cut
button on the Standard toolbar or by choosing **Edit | Cut**.

### Keyboard shortcuts

You may find it quicker to use Word's keyboard shortcuts for
copy, cut and paste operations as you need not take either
hand away from the keyboard:

- To copy, press Ctrl+c.   • To cut, press Ctrl+x.

- To paste, press Ctrl+v.

You can also right-click on your document to get a pop-up
menu displaying the available commands for copying,
cutting and pasting.

# Formatted documents

All Word documents are formatted, but some are more formatted
than others. In the remainder of this chapter you will discover
the Word tools that enable you to design a highly formatted
poster: indents, alignment, bullets, fonts, borders, and shading.

# Left and right indents

The term indent means 'in from the margin'. Word's indenting feature lets you push a paragraph of text a specified distance in from the left margin, right margin, or both.

To indent a selected paragraph, choose **Format | Paragraph**, and enter the required left and/or right distances on the Indents and Spacing tab of the Paragraph dialog box.

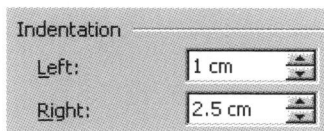

| Indentation | | |
|---|---|---|
| L̲eft: | 1 cm | ▲▼ |
| R̲ight: | 2.5 cm | ▲▼ |

In long documents, you may sometimes see indenting used as a way of attracting attention to a particular part of the text. Here is an example that combines a left and right indent with italics:

> *Another successful year has seen revenues rise by 35% and profits by 47.5%. Our company is well placed to face the challenges of the future.*

**Indent**
> *The positioning of a paragraph of text a specified distance in from the left and/or right margin.*

# Aligning text

To align text means to 'line up' the text in a particular horizontal (left-right) way. Word gives you four choices:

- **Left**: The default, used for letters and business documents. Left-aligned text is generally the easiest to read.

- **Centre**: Places the text between the left and right margins. Used for headings.

- **Right**: Aligns the text against the right-hand margin of the page. Used by graphic designers for decorative purposes.

- **Justify**: Both left and right-aligned at the same time. Used for narrow columns of text in newspapers and magazines.

Do not use justification when your text is in a single column across the width of the page (such as in letters), because it makes the text more difficult to read.

You can only align paragraphs. You cannot align selected characters or words within a paragraph.

To align a single paragraph, you don't need to select the text. You need only to position the cursor any place within the

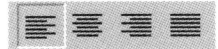

*Alignment buttons*

paragraph. You will find the four alignment buttons on the Formatting toolbar.

**Alignment**

> *The horizontal positioning of lines in a paragraph in relation to one another. They can share a common centre-point, begin at the same point on the left, end at the same point on the right, or begin and end at the same point.*

# Bullets and numbered lists

Lists are good ways to communicate a series of short statements or instructions. Lists are of two types:

- **Bulleted**: Used when the reading order is not critical. The bullet character is typically a dot, square, diamond, line or arrow. To make a bulleted list, select the paragraphs and click the Bullets button on the Formatting toolbar.

*Bullets button*

- **Numbered**: Used when the order of reading is important. For example, in directions and instructions. Each item is assigned a sequentially increasing number. To make a numbered list, select the paragraphs and click the Numbering button on the Formatting toolbar.

*Numbering button*

You can also make lists by choosing **Format | Bullets and Numbering**. Word offers you a wide range of options, such as the style of bullet or number character, and the distance between the bullet or number character and the bulleted or numbered text.

### Bulleted and numbered lists

*A list of short statements. The statements can be bulleted (preceded by a dot or other symbol) or numbered (preceded by a sequentially increasing number).*

Exercises 2.6, 2.7, and 2.8 take you through the steps of applying numbering and bullets to selected text.

### Exercise 2.6: Applying numbering to text

1  Open a new document, press the Caps Lock key once, type the following text:

MY FAVOURITE FRUIT

(The Caps Lock key is to the left of the letter 'a' key. After you press it, every letter you type is displayed as a capital letter.)

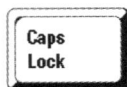

> Caps
> Lock

*Caps Lock key*

2   Press the Caps Lock key again to turn off capitals.

3   Select the text by clicking in front of the 'M' in My, and dragging to the right with the mouse.

MY·FAVOURITE·FRUIT¶          MY·FAVOURITE·FRUIT¶ I

*Click in front of the text ...*          *and drag the mouse to the right.*

4   Click the Underline button on the Formatting toolbar to underline the selected text.

MY·FAVOURITE·FRUIT¶
¶
Apples¶
Bananas¶
Grapes¶
Kiwis¶
Oranges¶
Peaches¶

5   Click the paragraph mark right of the text, and press Enter twice to create two new lines.

6   Type the following six fruit names, pressing Enter after each one: Apples, Bananas, Grapes, Kiwis, Oranges and Peaches. Your text should look as shown above right.

7   Select the six fruit names by clicking in front of the 'A' in Apples, and then dragging right and down with the mouse until you reach the final paragraph mark.

MY·FAVOURITE·FRUIT¶
¶
1.→Apples¶
2.→Bananas¶
3.→Grapes¶
4.→Kiwis¶
5.→Oranges¶
6.→Peaches¶

8   Click the Numbering button on the Formatting toolbar to applying numbering to the selected text.

9  Click anywhere in your document outside the selected area to deselect the text. Your text should now look as shown at the bottom of page 42.

(The arrows after the numbers are non-printing characters.)

10  Choose **File | Save** or press Ctrl+s to save your document. If your initials are KB, for example, name it KBList.doc. Leave the document open.

In Exercise 2.7 you will replace the numbers in Exercise 2.6 with bullets.

## Exercise 2.7: Applying bullets to text

1  Select the list of six fruit names that you entered in Exercise 2.6.

(Notice that you cannot select the numbers. Why? Because they are not entered text – they are generated automatically by Word.)

2  Click the Bullets button on the Formatting toolbar. Word replaces the numbers with bullets.

3  Choose **Format | Bullets and Numbering**, select the **Bulleted** tab, select one of the options, and then click **Customize**.

4  In the Text position area, change the value in the Indent at: box from the default to 1 cm, and click **OK**.

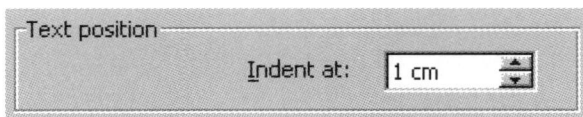

5   Click anywhere in your document outside the selected area to deselect the text.

Your text should now look as shown on the right.

(The arrows after the bullets are non-printing characters.)

MY·FAVOURITE·FRUIT¶
¶
•  →  Apples¶
•  →  Bananas¶
•  →  Grapes¶
•  →  Kiwis¶
•  →  Oranges¶
•  →  Peaches¶

Sometimes you want to apply bullets or numbering only to certain items in a list, and not to others. Exercise 2.8 provides an example.

## Exercise 2.8: Applying bullets to selected items in a list

1   Click at the paragraph mark after the words Kiwis, and press Enter to create a new line. Notice that Word places a bullet in front of the line.

2   Type the following:

(my absolute favourite)

3   You don't want this new line to have a bullet character in front of it.

Select the new line and click the Bullets button on the Formatting toolbar. Word removes the bullet format from the selected line.

4   Your final task is to align the new line with the other, bulleted lines.

With the new line still selected, choose **Format | Paragraph**, type a Left: indent of 1 cm, and click **OK**.

5 Click anywhere in your document outside the selected line to deselect it. Your text should now look as shown on the right.

This completes the bullets and numbering exercises.

Save and close your document.

MY·FAVOURITE·FRUIT¶
¶
- → Apples¶
- → Bananas¶
- → Grapes¶
- → Kiwis¶
  (my·absolute·favourite)¶
- → Oranges¶
- → Peaches¶

# Fonts

A font or typeface is a particular style of text. What fonts are installed on your computer? Click the arrow on the drop-down Font box on the Formatting toolbar to see.

Do you need to remember the names and characteristics of all these fonts? No. You need remember only two points about fonts:

- There are really just two kinds (families) of fonts: serif and sans serif. Sans serif just means without serifs.

- Serif fonts are good for long paragraphs of text (what is called body text). Sans serif fonts are good for short pieces of text such as headlines,

Times New Roman
- Bookman
- Bookman Old Style
- Braggadocio
- Bremen Bd BT
- Britannic Bold
- Brush Script MT
- Century Gothic
- Century Schoolbook
- Charlesworth
- Charting
- ChelthmITC Bk BT
- Clocks

*Viewing the fonts on your computer*

headers, captions, and maybe bulleted text.

You can recognize which family a font belongs to by asking: do its characters have serifs (tails or squiggles) at their edges?

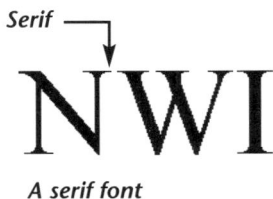

Serif ⎯⎯⎯⎯⎯⏋
                    ↓
# NWI

*A serif font*

# NWI

*Sans serif font*

## Serif fonts

Word's default font is a serif font called Times New Roman. It takes its name from *The Times* newspaper of London, where it was developed in the 1930s.

Other popular serif fonts include Garamond and Century Schoolbook:

This text is written in a font named Garamond.

This text is written in a font named Century Schoolbook.

## Sans serif fonts

Word's default sans serif font is Arial. It is based on another font, Helvetica. Other common sans serif fonts include Futura and Avant Garde:

This text is written in a font named Futura.

This text is written in a font named Avant Garde.

### Font

*A typeface: a particular style of text. The two main font families are serif and sans serif.*

# Font sizes

Font size is measured in a non-metric unit called the point, with approximately 72 points equal to one inch.

- For the body text of letters or longer business documents such as reports, 10, 11, or 12 points is a good choice. For headings, use larger font sizes in the range 14 to 28 points.

- Headers, footers, endnotes, footnotes, and captions are often in 8- or 9-point font size.

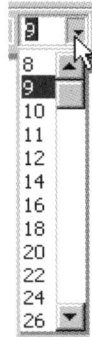

To change the font size of selected text, click the required font size from the Font Size drop-down list box on the Formatting toolbar.

# Font properties

Word's **Format | Font** dialog box enables you to apply a number of properties to fonts: style, effects, colour, and spacing.

### Font style

You have already applied these options using the Bold and Italic buttons on the Formatting toolbar.

### Underline

A lot of choices here. Single is both the simplest and the most commonly used. It is also the type of underline applied with the Underline button on the Formatting toolbar.

## Font colour

Do you have a colour printer? Then you may want to select a text colour other than Auto. Even without a colour printer, you may want to print your headings in grey.

What colour is Auto? Auto is black, unless the background is black or another dark colour, in which case Auto switches to white.

## Font effects

You can experiment with the various font effects by selecting any of the Effects checkboxes and viewing the result in the Preview area at the bottom of the dialog box.

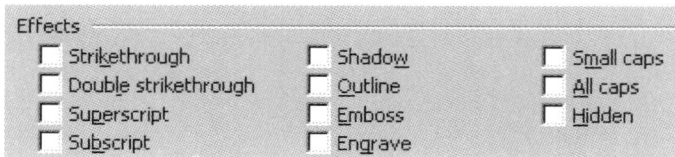

Effects

| | | |
|---|---|---|
| ☐ Strikethrough | ☐ Shadow | ☐ Small caps |
| ☐ Double strikethrough | ☐ Outline | ☐ All caps |
| ☐ Superscript | ☐ Emboss | ☐ Hidden |
| ☐ Subscript | ☐ Engrave | |

One important effect you need to know about is superscript.

This raises the selected text above the other text on the same line, and reduces its font size. It is used most commonly for mathematical symbols.

For example: $2^2$, $x^8$, $10^3$.

### Superscript

*Text that is raised above other text on the same line and is reduced in font size. Commonly used in maths texts for indices.*

The opposite of superscript is subscript. You will find subscripts used in the notation for chemical formulas.

For example: $H_2SO_4$

### Subscript

*Text that is lowered beneath other text on the same line is reduced in font size. Commonly used in chemistry texts for formulas.*

### Font spacing

You can expand or condense the space between characters by using the options on the Character Spacing tab of the Font dialog box.

Here is a line of text that is expanded by 1 point.

You may want to use this spacing effect for document headings.

# Font borders and shading

You can brighten up your document with borders (decorative boxes) and shading (coloured backgrounds), using the options available with the **Format | Borders and Shading** command.

Word offers a range of border settings, with Box and Shadow the most common choices. Use the Preview chapter on the right of the dialog box to select the edges that you want bordered. The default is all four edges.

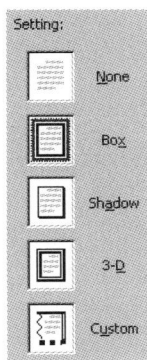

*Border options*

Pay attention to the Apply to: drop-down box at the bottom right. Your choice affects how Word draws the border. See the following example.

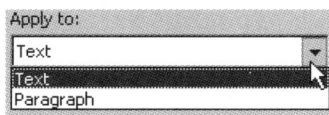

Apply to:

Text

Text
Paragraph

Sample·Text:·Apply·to·Text·Selected ¶

¶

Sample·Text:·Apply·to·Paragraph·Selected¶

To apply shading, select the text, choose **Format | Borders and Shading**, and then select your required Fill, Style, and Colour options from the Shading tab of the dialog box:

- **Fill:** This is the text background colour. If placing a grey shade behind black text, use 25% or less of grey. Otherwise, the text is difficult to read.

- **Style:** This allows you to apply tints (percentages of a colour) or patterns of a second colour (selected in the Colour box) on top of the selected Fill colour. Leave the Style: box at its default value of Clear if you do not want to apply a second colour.

- **Colour:** If you have selected a pattern in the Style box, select the colour of the lines and dots in the pattern here.

You can apply a border and shading to one or more characters, words or paragraphs. You need not apply both, but generally the border and shading features tend to be used together.

## Exercise 2.9: Designing your poster

Practice makes perfect. In this exercise you will apply the formatting (fonts, bullets, borders, and shading) and text positioning (alignment and indenting) skills that you have learned in this chapter. Your aim is to write and design a poster.

1 Open a new document and type the text shown below.

```
¶
Annual·Sale·of·Work¶
¶
In·aid·of·Local·Scout·Troop¶
¶
¶
Wheel·of·Fortune¶
Cakes¶
Books¶
Children's·Play·Area¶
¶
¶
¶
Where:¶
Local·Scout·Hall,·Main·Street¶
¶
When:¶
2pm¶
Sunday,·17·October¶
¶
Admission·Free¶
¶
All·Welcome¶¶
```

**2** Select the text: Annual Sale of Work. Using **Format |
Font**, make it Times New Roman, 28 point.

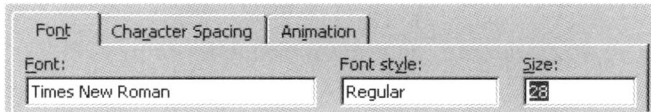

| Fo<u>n</u>t | Cha<u>r</u>acter Spacing | Ani̲mation |
|---|---|---|

| <u>F</u>ont: | Font st<u>y</u>le: | <u>S</u>ize: |
|---|---|---|
| Times New Roman | Regular | 28 |

**3** Choose **Format | Borders and Shading**, select a
Setting: of Box and select Text as the Apply to: option.

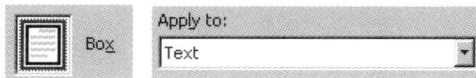

| | Bo<u>x</u> | App<u>l</u>y to: |
|---|---|---|
| | | Text |

**4** On the Shading tab,
select a shading of 15%
grey. When finished,
click **OK**.

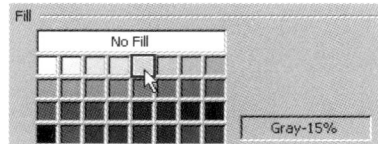

Fill
No Fill

Gray-15%

**5** Select the text: In aid of Local Scout Troop. Use the
options on the Formatting toolbar to centre-align it, and
make it Arial Black, 14 point.

| Arial Black | ▼ | 14 | ▼ |
|---|---|---|---|

**6** Select the four attractions: Wheel of
Fortune, Cakes, Books, and Children's
Play Area. Make them Arial, 20 point.

(Ensure the paragraph mark after Children's
Play Area is included in your selection.)

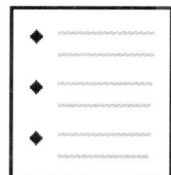

Choose **Format | Bullets and
Numbering**. On the Bulleted tab, select
the diamond bullet character style. (You
may have to click **Customize** to find this option.)

*Diamond style
bullet character*

**7** You want to place the bullets where they will get attention: in the centre of the page between the left and right page margins.

◆ → Wheel·of·Fortune¶
◆ → Cakes¶
◆ → Books¶
◆ → Children's·Play·Area¶

But do not apply centre-alignment, as shown above, as the bullets are easier to read if they are left-aligned.

With the four attractions still selected, select **Format | Paragraph** and apply a left indent of 4.5 cm.

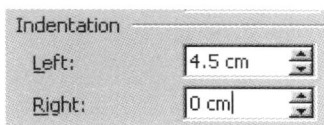

| Indentation | |
|---|---|
| Left: | 4.5 cm |
| Right: | 0 cm |

Your bulleted text remains left-aligned, but is now in the centre of the page.

**8** Select all the text above the four bullet points, and make it centre-aligned, Arial, Regular, 20 point.

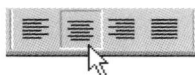

Arial ▾ 20 ▾

**9** Repeat Step 8 for all the text below the four bullet points.

**10** Select each of the following words in turn and click the Bold button on the Formatting toolbar:

Where:, When:, and Admission Free.

**11** Select the words All Welcome and click the Italics button on the Formatting toolbar.

**12** Finally, with the cursor positioned anywhere on the page, choose **Format | Borders and Shading**, and select the Page Border tab.

Select a Setting: of Box and, in the Apply to: field, select Whole Document, and click **OK**.

| Box | Apply to: |
|-----|-----------|
| | Whole document ▼ |

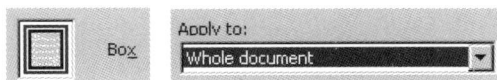

Your poster is now complete and should look like the sample shown. Save your poster with a name that you will find easy to remember and recognize. If your initials are KB, for example, save the poster document as KBposter.doc.

If you have a printer, print out your poster and inspect your work!

## Annual Sale of Work

**In aid of Local Scout Troop**

- ◆ Wheel of Fortune
- ◆ Cakes
- ◆ Books
- ◆ Children's Play Area

**Where:**
Local Scout Hall, Main Street

**When:**
2pm,
Sunday, 17 October

**Admission Free**

*All Welcome*

# Word's Zoom views

Word's Zoom feature enables you to magnify or reduce the document display. You can use Zoom in either of two ways:

- Click in the Zoom box on the Standard toolbar, enter a number between 10% and 500%, and press Enter.

*Zoom box*

- Choose **View | Zoom**, and select a magnification or reduction option from the Zoom dialog box.

To return from an enlarged or reduced view to normal view, select a magnification of 100% – or click the Undo button on the Standard toolbar.

## Zoom and printing

The Zoom feature affects only the way that Word displays a document on-screen – and not how a document is printed. (You will learn about printing documents in Chapter 3.)

# Saving to a diskette

Have you been saving your documents as you went along? You should. It is also a good idea to save a copy of your document to a diskette. Follow the steps in Exercise 2.10 to learn how to save your poster to the A: drive.

### Exercise 2.10: Saving a Word document to a diskette

1  Insert a diskette in the diskette drive of your computer:

- If it is a new diskette, ensure that it is formatted.

- If it is a previously used one, ensure that there is sufficient space on it to hold the Word document file. Your poster file should be around 60 KB in size.

2  Choose **File | Save As**, locate the A: drive, and click **Save** to save the file. Word suggests the default file name (in this example, KBposter.doc) for you to accept or amend.

When finished, use **File | Save As** again to resave the document to its original location on your computer.

If you do not, saving the file in future (by clicking the Save button on the Standard toolbar or choosing **File | Save**) will save the work to the diskette – and not to the hard disk in your computer.

# Symbols and special characters

Word allows you to insert symbols and special characters in your documents:

- **Symbols**: Among the symbols are foreign language letters with accents (such as á, é, ä, and ë), fractions, and characters used in science and mathematics.

- **Special Characters**: These include the copyright (©), registered (®) and trademark (™) symbols, plus typographic characters such as the en dash (a short dash the width of the letter 'n'), the em dash (a longer dash the width of the letter 'm'), and various types of opening and closing quotes.

To insert a symbol or special character:

- Click where you want to insert the symbol.

- Choose **Insert | Symbol**, and then click the Symbols or Special Characters tab.

- Double-click the symbol or character you want to insert.

- Click **Close** to close the dialog box.

# Format painter

Word's Format Painter provides a quick, convenient way to copy formatting from one piece of text to another. Follow these steps:

- Select the text that has the formatting you want to copy.

  *Format Painter button*

- Click the Format Painter button on the Standard toolbar.

- Select the text to which you want to apply the formatting.

To copy the selected formatting to several locations, double-click Format Painter.

When you have finished copying the formatting, click the Format Painter button again or press the Esc key at the top-left of your keyboard.

## Exercise 2.11: Copying formatting

You begin this exercise by removing the formatting from two lines of your Annual Sale of Work poster.

**1** Is the poster document from Exercise 2.9 open? If not, open it now.

**2** Select the text 'Where:', choose **Format | Font,** make it 10 point, Regular, Times New Roman, and click **OK.**

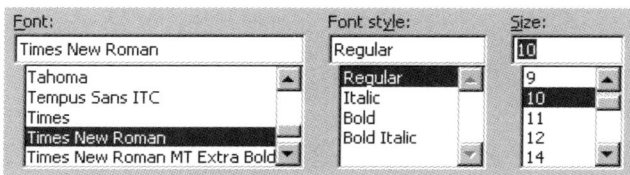

| Font: | Font style: | Size: |
|---|---|---|
| Times New Roman | Regular | 10 |
| Tahoma | Regular | 9 |
| Tempus Sans ITC | Italic | 10 |
| Times | Bold | 11 |
| Times New Roman | Bold Italic | 12 |
| Times New Roman MT Extra Bold | | 14 |

**3** Select the text 'When:'. Also make it 10 point, Regular, Times New Roman.

In the next part of this exercise, you will copy the formatting from another part of the poster to the two lines whose formatting you removed in steps 2 and 3 above.

**4** Click anywhere in the words 'Admission Free'.

**5** Double-click the Format Painter button.

**6** Select the text 'Where:'

**7** Select the text 'When:'

**8** Press the Esc key to switch off the Format Painter feature.

Your poster now looks as it did before this exercise. Save the poster and close it. You can also close Microsoft Word. You have now completed Chapter 2 of the ECDL *Word Processing* module.

# Chapter summary: so now you know

Before you format or align text, you must first select that text. You do so by clicking and then dragging with the mouse. Word displays selected text in reverse (white text on black background).

Bold, italic, and underline are Word's most commonly used *formatting* features. Buttons for these options are provided on the Formatting toolbar.

You can *copy* text from one part of a document and then paste it to another part (or even to a different document) using the *clipboard*, a temporary storage area. You can also *cut and paste* text, in which case Word deletes the text from its original location.

*Indenting* is a way of moving text a specified distance in from the left or right margin of the page – or from both. *Alignment* is a way of positioning text in a paragraph so it lines up beside the left margin, beside the right margin, beside both left and right margins (*justification*) or an equal distance from both left and right margins (*centred*). Buttons for the alignment options are provided on the Formatting toolbar.

Use lists to communicate short statements or instructions. *Bulleted lists*, in which each item is preceded by a symbol such as a square or diamond, are suitable when the reading order is not critical. *Numbered lists*, in which each item is preceded by a sequentially increasing number, are used for instructions and directions, where the order of reading is important.

*Fonts* (typefaces) are styles of text. Serif fonts are better for long paragraphs. Use sans serif fonts for shorter text items, such as headlines or captions. Two important font effects are *superscript* (used for writing mathematical indices) and *subscript* (used for writing chemical formulas).

You can brighten up your documents by adding decorative borders and background *shading*.

Word's *Zoom* feature enables you to magnify or reduce the document display – without affecting how the document is printed.

You can insert *symbols* and *special characters* in a document to represent such items as foreign language letters with accents, fractions, characters used in scientific and mathematical texts, and typographic characters such as dashes and quotes.

Word's *Format Painter* provides a quick, convenient way to copy formatting from one piece of text to another.

# CHAPTER 3

# Long documents, little details

## In this chapter

Both for the writer and reader, long documents present problems that shorter ones do not. Word offers features to make life easier for both.

To help you edit long documents, Word includes a spell-checker, a grammar-checker, and a find-and-replace feature.

You can help readers navigate their way through long documents by inserting page numbers and other details in the header or footer.

Also in this chapter, you will discover how to control vertical spacing between lines and paragraphs, how to create new types of indents to highlight breaks between paragraphs, and how to insert line and page breaks.

## New skills

At the end of this chapter you should be able to:

- Change the spacing between lines and between paragraphs
- Apply a first-line indent to a paragraph
- Apply a hanging indent to a paragraph
- Find and replace text, formatting, and special characters
- Adjust page margins and page orientation
- Create and format headers and footers
- Insert page numbers and document details in a header or footer
- Insert manual line breaks and page breaks
- Use Word's spell- and grammar-checkers
- Use Word's printing options

## New words

At the end of this chapter you should be able to explain the following terms:

- Inter-line spacing
- Margin
- Inter-paragraph spacing
- A4
- First-line indent
- Header and footer
- Hanging indent

# Creating your long document

To learn how to work with long documents in Word, you need a sample long document to practise on. You begin this chapter by copying some text from Word's online help.

## Exercise 3.1: Copying text from Word online help

1   Open Word and choose **Help | Microsoft Word Help**. On the Contents tab of the Help Topics dialog box, double-click the topic: Working with Long Documents.

2   Word displays a list of sub-topics. Double-click on: Automatically Summarizing a Document. You are shown a further sub-listing. Double-click on: About automatically summarizing a document.

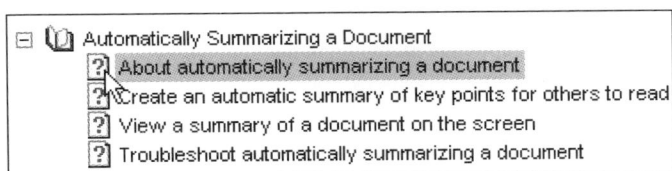

3   On the help screen displayed, select the two paragraphs of text shown below by dragging the mouse over them.

---

**What is AutoSummarize?**

AutoSummarize identifies the key points in a document for you to share with others or quickly scan.

AutoSummarize determines key points by analyzing the document and assigning a score to each sentence. Sentences that contain words used frequently in the document are given a higher score. You then choose a percentage of the highest-scoring sentences to display in the summary.

AutoSummarize works best on well-structured documents such as reports, articles, and scientific papers.

Return to top

---

4   Right-click on the selected text, choose **Copy** from the pop-up menu, and close the online help window by clicking on the close box in the top-right corner.

5   Click the New button on the Standard toolbar to create a new Word document, and choose **Edit | Paste** to paste the online help text into the new document.

---

AutoSummarize·identifies·the·key·points·in·a·document·for·you·to·share·with·others·or· quickly·scan.¶

AutoSummarize·determines·key·points·by·analyzing·the·document·and·assigning·a·score· to·each·sentence.·Sentences·that·contain·words·used·frequently·in·the·document·are·given· a·higher·score.·You·then·choose·a·percentage·of·the·highest-scoring·sentences·to·display· in·the·summary.¶

¶

---

6   Delete the 'spare' paragraph mark at the end of the new document by clicking on it and pressing the Backspace key.

7   Move the cursor to the start of the first line of the first paragraph. Press Enter to create a new line, and move the cursor up to the start of that line.

---

¶

AutoSummarize·identifies·the·key·points·in·a·document·for·you·to·share·with·others·or· quickly·scan.¶

---

8   Type the following: Heading One

Heading·One¶  I

AutoSummarize·identifies·the·key·points·in·a·document·for·you·to·share·with·others·or·
quickly·scan.¶

9   Hold down the Ctrl key and click in the left margin of
    the page where there is no text. This selects all the text
    in the document.

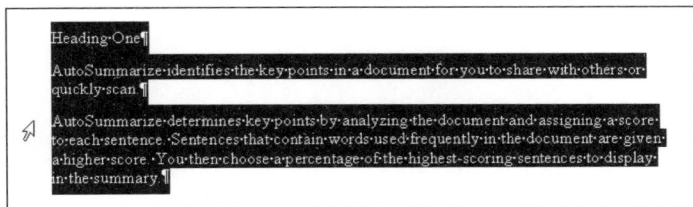

Heading·One¶

AutoSummarize·identifies·the·key·points·in·a·document·for·you·to·share·with·others·or·
quickly·scan.¶

AutoSummarize·determines·key·points·by·analyzing·the·document·and·assigning·a·score·
to·each·sentence.·Sentences·that·contain·words·used·frequently·in·the·document·are·given·
a·higher·score.·You·then·choose·a·percentage·of·the·highest-scoring·sentences·to·display·
in·the·summary.¶

10  Choose **Edit | Copy** to copy the text to the clipboard.
    Deselect the text by clicking anywhere on the page
    outside the selected text.

11  Move the cursor down to the end of the second
    paragraph, and press Enter twice to move down the
    cursor a further two lines.

a·higher·score.·You·then·choose·a·percentage·of·the·highest-scoring·sentences·to·display·
in·the·summary.¶  I

¶

¶

12  The text you copied in step 10 is still in the clipboard.
    Choose **Edit | Paste** to paste it again.

13  Repeat steps 11 and 12 fifteen times to create three
    pages of sample text.

14  Choose **File | Save** to save the document with a name
    that you will find easy to remember. If your initials are
    KB, for example, call it KBlong.doc.

Congratulations! You have created a three-page document in Word without typing a single line of text! You will use this sample document in other exercises in this chapter.

# Inter-line spacing

Inter-line spacing is the vertical space between lines within a paragraph of text. By default, Word applies single inter-line spacing. You can increase the inter-line spacing of a selected paragraph by choosing **Format | Paragraph**, and, in the Line Spacing: box, selecting 1.5 lines or Double.

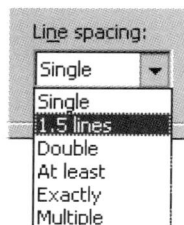

Line spacing:

| Single | ▼ |
|---|---|
| Single | |
| 1.5 lines | |
| Double | |
| At least | |
| Exactly | |
| Multiple | |

Alternatively, enter a font size in the At: box, and select At Least: in the Line Spacing box. A good rule is to make inter-line spacing one point size larger than the font size. If your text is 10 points, for example, make inter-line spacing 11 points.

### Inter-line spacing

*The vertical space between lines within a paragraph of text. Word's default is single-line spacing.*

*Examples of single, 1.5 and double inter-line spacing*

| | | |
|---|---|---|
| How·does·AutoS document·and·as that·contain·worc scoring·sentence ¶ Keep·in·mind·tha reports,·articles,·: ¶ How·does·AutoS document·and·as that·contain·worc scoring·sentence that·contain·worc scoring·sentence | How·does·AutoSu document·and·assi that·contain·words scoring·sentences· ¶ Keep·in·mind·that· reports,·articles,·ai ¶ How·does·AutoSu | How·does·AutoS document·and·as that·contain·worc scoring·sentence: ¶ Keep·in·mind·tha reports,·articles,·: |

# Inter-paragraph spacing

Pressing the Enter key to add a blank line between paragraphs of text is a crude – if effective – way of controlling the inter-paragraph spacing (spacing between paragraphs) in your documents.

For longer documents, you may instead wish to use the **Format | Paragraph** command, and enter an inter-paragraph space value in the Space Before: and/or Space After: boxes:

- For body text, enter a Space After: (slightly larger than the text font size) to separate the next paragraph from the current one.

- For headings, enter a value in the Space Before: box to place an extra area of blank space above the headings. This helps your headings to stand out from the rest of the text.

*Inter-paragraph spacing, created with and without extra paragraph marks*

| | |
|---|---|
| How·does·AutoSı document·and·ass that·contain·word scoring·sentences ¶ Keep·in·mind·that reports,·articles,·a ¶ How·does·AutoSı document·and·ass that·contain·word scoring·sentences | How·does·AutoSı document·and·ass that·contain·word scoring·sentences Keep·in·mind·thaı reports,·articles,·a How·does·AutoSı document·and·ass that·contain·word scoring·sentences |

**Inter-paragraph spacing**
*The spacing between successive paragraphs of text.*

Another option for long documents is to set inter-paragraph spacing for body text to zero, and to use instead first-line indenting as a way of indicating where each new paragraph begins. See the next topic.

# First-line indents

In Chapter 2 you learned how to indent a selected paragraph from the left and/or right margins of the page. Word also lets you indent the first line of a paragraph only, so that it starts a greater distance in from the left margin than the other lines of the same paragraph.

### Exercise 3.2: Creating a first-line indent

Here you will use a first-line indent to separate two paragraphs of body text.

**1** Select the second paragraph of your sample text.

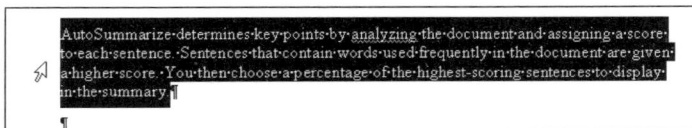

AutoSummarize·determines·key·points·by·analyzing·the·document·and·assigning·a·score·
to·each·sentence.·Sentences·that·contain·words·used·frequently·in·the·document·are·given·
a·higher·score.·You·then·choose·a·percentage·of·the·highest-scoring·sentences·to·display·
in·the·summary.¶

¶

**2** Choose **Format | Paragraph**.

**3** On the Indents and Spacing tab, in the Special: box, select First line. In the By: box, enter a value of 1 cm. Click **OK**.

Special:        By:
First line  ▾   1 cm  ⬍

Your text should now look as shown.

> AutoSummarize·determines·key·points·by·analyzing·the·document·and·assigning·a·score·to·each·sentence. ·Sentences·that·contain·words·used·frequently·in·the·document·are·given·a·higher·score. ·You·then·choose·a·percentage·of·the·highest-scoring·sentences·to·display·in·the·summary.¶
>
> ¶

**4**  Undo the first-line indent change by choosing **Edit | Undo Paragraph Formatting**. Your sample text should look as it was before this exercise.

### First-line indent

*The positioning of the first line of a paragraph a greater distance in from the left margin than the remaining lines of the same paragraph.*

If using first-line indents to separate paragraphs, set inter-paragraph spacing to zero or to just 1 or 2 points. Do not use first-line indents for the first paragraph after a heading.

## Hanging indents

A hanging indent is where all the lines of a paragraph are indented – except the first one. Hanging indents are sometimes used for lists such as bibliographies. Below is an example.

> *The·Memoirs·of·James·II* ·Translated·by·A. ·Lytton·Sells·from·the·Bouillon·Manuscript. ·Edited·and·collated·with·the·Clarke·Edition. ·With·an·introduction·by·Sir·Arthur·Bryant.¶
>
> *The·History·of·England·from·the·Accession·of·James·II.* ·Lord·Macauley,·edited·by·Lady·Tevelyan.¶

Practise creating a hanging
indent with the sample text by
selecting a paragraph, choosing
**Format | Paragraph**, selecting Hanging from the Special:
box, and entering a value in the By: box. Undo any changes
that you make.

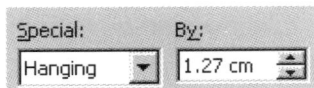

### Hanging indent

*Where all the lines of a paragraph are indented – except
the first one. Sometimes used for lists.*

# Finding text

Do you need to locate quickly a particular word or phrase in a
long document? Word's Find feature can take you straight to
the text that you are looking for.

By default, Word searches the whole document. To limit
the text that Word searches through, first select only that part
of the document. When Word has finished searching the
selected text, it asks whether you want to search the
remainder of the document or not.

### The basics

Choose **Edit | Find** to display the Find and Replace dialog
box. In the Find what: box, type (or paste in from the
clipboard) the text you want to find, and choose **Find Next**.

**Find and Replace**

Find | Replace | Go To

Find what: the

Options: Search Down

More ▼ | Find Next | Cancel

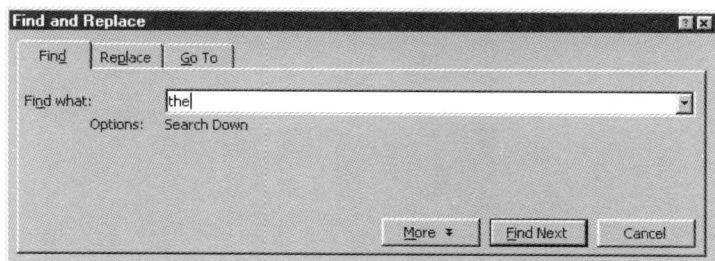

Word takes you to the first occurrence of the search text in your document. The dialog box stays open on your screen. Click **Find Next** to continue searching for further occurrences, or click **Cancel** to close the dialog box and end your search. Practise by searching for the word 'the' in your sample document.

## Special options

By default, Word finds parts of words as well as whole words. When you search for 'the', Word also finds 'then'. You can tell Word to find whole words only by clicking the **More** button, and then selecting the Find whole words only checkbox.

More ▼

☐ Match case
☑ Find whole words only
☐ Use wildcards
☑ Sounds like
☐ Find all word forms

Another option is to select the Match case checkbox. So, for example, a search for 'The' does not find 'the' or 'THE'.

To find paragraph marks, tabs or other special or non-printing characters, choose the **Special** button and click on the relevant character.

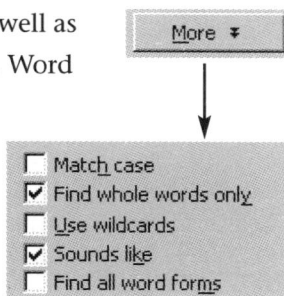

## Formats

You can tell Word to find only occurrences of text that is in a certain format. Click the **Format** button, and select the formatting option that you require.

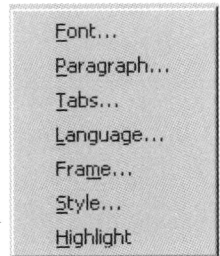

| Font... |
| Paragraph... |
| Tabs... |
| Language... |
| Frame... |
| Style... |
| Highlight |

Format ▾ ⟶

# Finding and replacing text

Sometimes you will want to find and replace all occurrences of a word or phrase in a document with a different word or phrase. You might have misspelled a word consistently throughout a document, for example, or maybe you want to substitute 'person' for 'man' or 'woman'.

To replace text, choose **Edit | Replace**. On the Replace tab, enter the text you want to replace in the Find what: box, and the new text you want to substitute for the replaced text in the Replace with: box.

## The two replace methods

You are offered two options by the Replace tab of the Find and Replace dialog box.

- Word replaces your text one occurrence at a time. At each occurrence, you are asked whether you want to make the replacement or not. This is the 'safe' option.

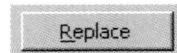

Replace

- Word replaces all
  occurrences in a single

  | Replace All |

  operation. Use this
  option only if you are certain that you want to replace
  every instance of the text you are searching for!

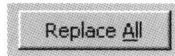

## Special options

Anything that you can locate with the **Find** command, you
can replace with **Edit | Find and Replace** – including
formatting, tabs, and other special and non-printing
characters.

### Exercise 3.3: Finding and replacing text

In this exercise you will practise finding and replacing
text in your sample long document.

1   Look at the second of the two paragraphs that you
    pasted in from the online help text.

    Copy the following to the clipboard: analyzing

2   Move the cursor to the start of the first line of the
    document. Choose **Edit | Replace**.

3   On the Replace tab, paste the copied text in the Find
    what: box.

    | Find what: | analyzing | ▼ |

4   Type this in the Replace with: box: analysing

| Replace with: | analysing | ▾ |
|---|---|---|

5  Click the **Replace All** button.

Word performs the find-and-replace operation through the entire document. So much easier than correcting each occurrence of the error!

6  When finished, Word displays a dialog box similar to the one shown. Click **OK** to close this dialog box.

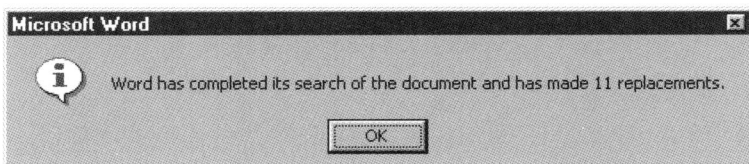

**Microsoft Word**                                                      ☒

ⓘ    Word has completed its search of the document and has made 11 replacements.

OK

7  Close the Find and Replace dialog box by clicking **Close**.

## Exercise 3.4: Finding and replacing formatting

In this exercise you will use Word's find and replace feature to reformat all occurrences of a heading in your sample long document.

1  Move the cursor to the start of the first line of the document. Choose **Edit | Replace**.

2  On the Replace tab, notice that the Find what: box still contains the text from Exercise 3.3. Click in the Find what: box, delete the previous text, and type the following: Heading One

3  Click in the Replace with: box, delete the text from Exercise 3.3, and type the following: Heading One

**4** With the cursor in the Replace: box, click the **More** button and then the **Format** button.

**5** Select the Font option, and specify a Font of Arial, a Font Style of Bold, and a Size of 14. Then click **OK**.

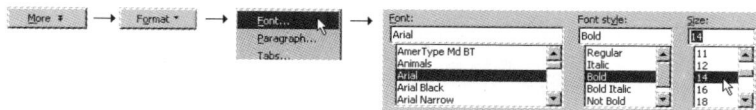

**6** Click the **Replace All** button.

Word reformats every occurrence of the heading. Click **OK** to accept the replacements and click **Close** to close the dialog box.

## Exercise 3.5: Finding and replacing special characters

In this exercise you will remove the extra paragraph mark that separates the paragraphs of the sample text.

**1** Move the cursor to the start of the first line of the document. Choose **Edit | Replace**.

**2** On the Replace tab, click in the Find what: box and delete the text from Exercise 3.4.

**3** With the cursor in the Find what: box, click the **Special** button and select Paragraph Mark from the pop-up menu. Click **Special** a second time and again click Paragraph Mark.

The Find what: box should contain Word's paragraph mark symbol twice (^p^p).

| Find what: | ^p^p | ▾ |
|---|---|---|

4   Click in the Replace with box: and delete the text from
Exercise 3.4. Also, click **No Formatting** to remove the
formatting that you specified in Exercise 3.4.

5   With the cursor in the Replace with: box, click the
**Special** button and select Paragraph Mark from the
pop-up menu.

| Replace with: | ^p| | ▾ |
|---|---|---|

6   Click **Replace All**.

Word replaces all occurrences of two consecutive
paragraph marks with a single paragraph mark. Click
**OK** to accept the replacements and click **Close** to close
the dialog box.

## Exercise 3.6: Finding and replacing text positioning

In this exercise you will apply a first-line indent to all
occurrences of the second paragraph of sample text.

1   Move the cursor to the start of the first line of the
document. Choose **Edit | Replace**.

2   On the Replace tab, click in the Find what: box. Delete
the text from Exercise 3.5 and type the first two words
of the second paragraph of the sample text:

AutoSummarize determines

(Because both paragraphs begin with the same word, we use an additional word to ensure that only the second paragraph is selected.)

3   Click in the Replace with: box, delete the text from Exercise 3.5, and type the same words as are in the Find what: box.

4   With the cursor still in the Replace with: box, click the **Format** button (you may have to click the **More** button first to find this), then the **Paragraph** option, and specify a first-line indent of 1 cm. Click **OK**.

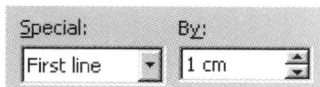

| Special: | By: |
|---|---|
| First line | 1 cm |

The Find and Replace dialog box should look as shown.

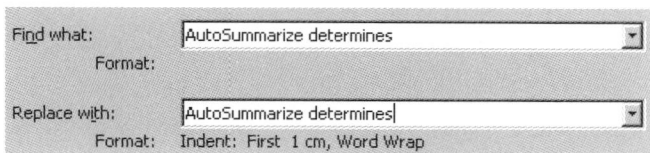

| Find what: | AutoSummarize determines |
|---|---|
| Format: | |
| Replace with: | AutoSummarize determines |
| Format: | Indent: First 1 cm, Word Wrap |

5   Click **Replace All**.

Word indents the first line of every occurrence of the second paragraph.

6   Click **OK** to accept the replacements and click **Close** to close the dialog box. Your document should look like the sample shown. (The inter-line and inter-paragraph spacing may be different on your PC.)

---

**Heading·One¶**

AutoSummarize·identifies·the·key·points·in·a·document·for·you·to·share·with·others·or· quickly·scan.¶

    AutoSummarize·determines·key·points·by·analysing·the·document·and·assigning·a· score·to·each·sentence.·Sentences·that·contain·words·used·frequently·in·the·document·are· given·a·higher·score.·You·then·choose·a·percentage·of·the·highest-scoring·sentences·to· display·in·the·summary.¶

You have completed the find-and-replace exercises. Save your long document and leave it open.

# Page setup

You have learnt how to control where text appears on the printed page, using text alignment, indenting, inter-line spacing and inter-paragraph spacing.

But what about the page on which the text appears? What options does Word offer you?

Choose **File | Page Setup** to view the four tabs of page setup options. Only two of these tabs are relevant at this stage: Margins and Paper Size.

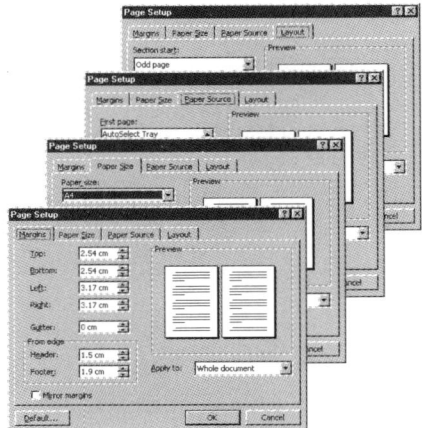

### The Margins tab

A margin is the distance that the text and graphics are positioned in from the edge of the printed page.

Word's default margin values – top and bottom, 1 inch (2.54 cm), left and right, 1.25 inches (3.17 cm) – are acceptable for most letters and business documents.

*Margins indicated
by dashed lines*

You can change the margins at any stage, and make your new values the new defaults by clicking the **Default** button.

### Margin

*The distance of the text and graphics from the edge of the printed page. Word lets you specify separate top, bottom, left, and right margins.*

### Paper size

For the Paper size: box, accept the default of A4. This is the European standard paper size (21 cm wide and 29.7 cm high). A4 pages are used for almost all letters and other business documents.

### A4

*The standard page size for letters and most other business documents throughout Europe.*

Orientation is the direction in which the page is printed. Your options are Portrait ('standing up') and Landscape ('on its side'). Letters and most other business documents are printed in portrait.

## Headers and footers

Headers and footers are pieces of text that appear on the top and bottom of every page of a document (except the title and contents pages).

Looking at examples of published documents, you will see that headers and footers typically contain such details as document title, organization name, author name, and perhaps a version or draft number. Usually, headers and footers also contain page numbers. You will learn about page numbering in the next topic.

*Word places headers and footers in the top and bottom page margins, set with the File|Page Setup command*

With Word, you need only type in header and/or footer text once, and the program repeats the text on every page. Any formatting that you can apply to text in your document – such as bold, italics, alignment, borders and shading – you can also apply to text in the headers and footers. You can also insert graphics, such as a company logo, in a header and footer.

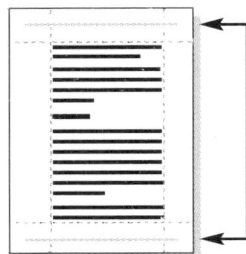

### Headers and footers

*Standard text and graphics that are printed in the top and bottom margins of every page of a document.*

Here are a few facts about headers and footers in Word:

- You insert them with the **View | Header and Footer** command.

- This command displays the header or footer area (surrounded by a dashed border), the document text (which you cannot edit when working with headers and footers), and a Header and Footer toolbar (giving you quick access to the commonly used commands).

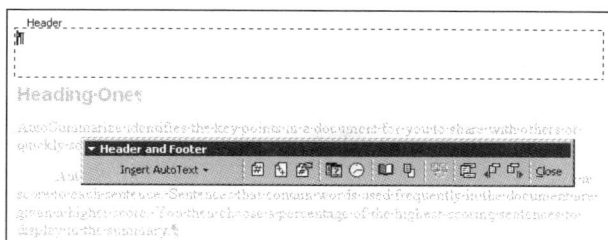

*Word's header area with toolbar*

- Word positions the paragraph mark at the left of the header or footer area, ready for you to type text.

- Word inserts two preset tab stops to make it easy for you to centre-align or right-align headers or footers. Press Tab once to centre a header or footer, press Tab twice to line it up against the right margin.

*Switch Between Header and Footer button*

- Click the Switch between Header and Footer button to view the footer area when in the header area, and vice versa. The two areas are similar in appearance and operation.

- Place page numbers (discussed in the next topic) at the outside margin (left for left-hand side pages, right for right-hand pages) or at the centre of the header or footer area.

- Place text at the centre or at the inside margin of the header or footer area.

## Exercise 3.7: Creating a header

In this exercise you will insert header text in your sample document.

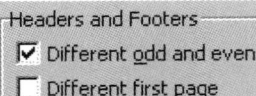

> **Headers and Footers**
> ☑ Different o̲dd and even
> ☐ Different f̲irst page

1   Choose **File | Page Setup**, select the **Layout** tab, ensure that the Header and Footer checkboxes are as shown above right, and click **OK**.

2   Choose **View | Header and Footer**. Word positions the paragraph mark at the left of the header area, ready for you to type text.

3   Type the following text: Annual Report

```
Odd Page Header
Annual·Report¶
```

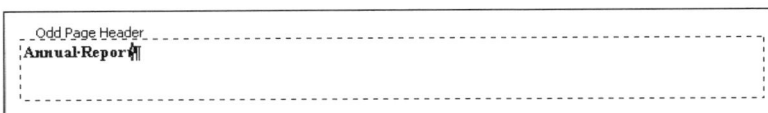

4   Click the Show Next button on the Header and Footer toolbar. Word takes you to the next page, the first even (left-hand) page of the document.

5   Press the Tab key twice to move the paragraph mark against the right-hand margin. Type the following text: ABC Limited

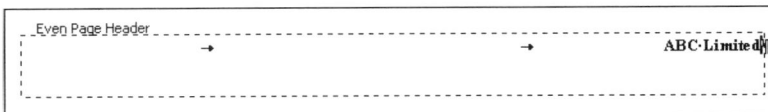

```
Even Page Header
                →                    →            ABC·Limited¶
```

6   Click the Close button on the right of the Header and Footer toolbar. Save your document.

Because you began this exercise by selecting the Different odd and even: checkbox on **File | Setup**, Word allowed you to type separate headers for odd (right-hand) and even (left-hand) pages.

In the next exercise you will place a border under the header text to help separate it from the main body of the document. You will also change the font and font size. Typically, the header font is 2 or 3 point sizes smaller than the body text. At that size, sans serif fonts such as Arial are easier to read than serif ones.

### Exercise 3.8: Formatting a header

1   Display the first page of your document and choose **View | Header and Footer**.

2   Select the header text.

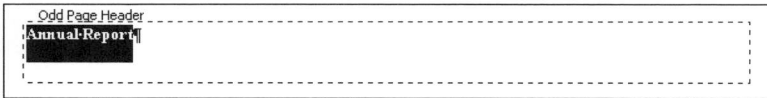

3   Chose **Format | Font**, and select Arial, Regular, 8 point.

4   With the text still selected, choose **Format | Borders and Shading**.

5   On the Borders tab, do the following:

   • Select None for Setting.

   • In the Preview area of the dialog box, click on the Apply to: drop-down list and select Paragraph.

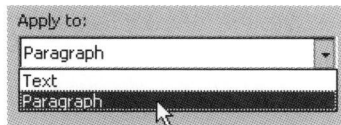

- Also in the Preview area, click the Border Beneath button.

- Finally, click **OK** to close the dialog box and apply the header border.

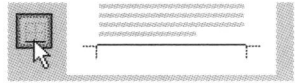

6   Click the Show Next button on the Header and Footer toolbar. Repeat Steps 2 to 5 for the left-hand page.

7   Click the Close button on the Header and Footer toolbar.

The top of your right-hand pages should now look as below.

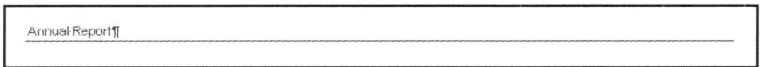

Annual Report¶

The top of your left-hand pages should now look as below.

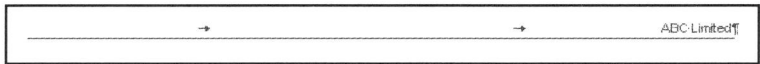

ABC·Limited¶

Notice that the header text is 'greyed out', indicating that you cannot edit it when working with the main body of the document.

# Page numbering

You can insert a page number in the header or footer of a document. Word updates the page numbers as you add or remove document pages. The same formatting options are available for the page number as for header and footer text. You can align a page number at the left or right margin, or in the centre of the header or footer area.

## Exercise 3.9: Inserting a page number

In this exercise you will insert a centre-aligned page number in the footer of your sample document.

1   Display the first page of your document, choose **View |
    Header and Footer**, and click the Switch between
    Header and Footer button.

2   Click in the footer area, and press the Tab key once to
    move the cursor to the centre-aligned position.

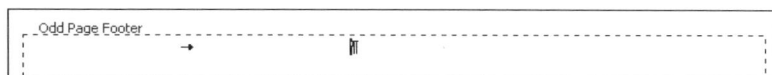

```
 _Odd Page Footer_____
 |              →                    ¶                          |
 |                                                              |
```

3   Click the Insert Page Number button on the
    Header and Footer toolbar. Word inserts the
    page number and displays it against a
    grey background.

*Insert Page
Number button*

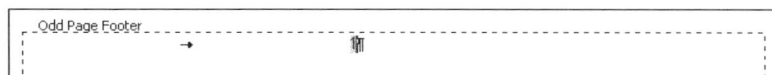

```
 _Odd Page Footer_____
 |              →                    1¶                         |
 |                                                              |
```

4   Click the Show Next button on the Header and Footer
    toolbar to move to the second page, the first even (left-
    hand) page of your document.

5   Repeat steps 2 and 3 to insert the page number in the
    centre-aligned position.

6   Click the Close button on the Header and Footer
    toolbar. Save your document.

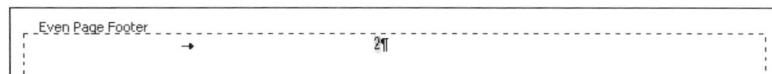

```
 _Even Page Footer_____
 |              →                    2¶                         |
 |                                                              |
```

### Page-numbering options

Click on the Format Page Number button on the
Header and Footer toolbar to display the page-
numbering options.

*Format Page
Number button*

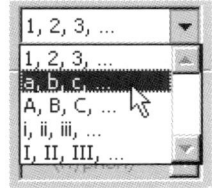

You can number the pages using
numbers, letters, or Roman numerals. And
you can start at a number other than one.

| 1, 2, 3, ... |
|---|
| 1, 2, 3, ... |
| a, b, c, |
| A, B, C, ... |
| i, ii, iii, ... |
| I, II, III, ... |

Start at:    10

# Document date and author name

Word offers special features to make it easier for you to insert
today's date and your name in a header or footer.

**Document creation date**

To insert today's date (as recorded on your computer) in a
header or footer, follow these steps:

* Choose **View | Header and Footer**.

* Position the cursor where you want to insert
the current date.

* Click the Date button on the Header and
Footer toolbar.

*Date button*

**Document author name**

To insert the author's name (that is, your name), follow
these steps:

* Choose **File | Properties**, and check that your name is
displayed in the Author: box.

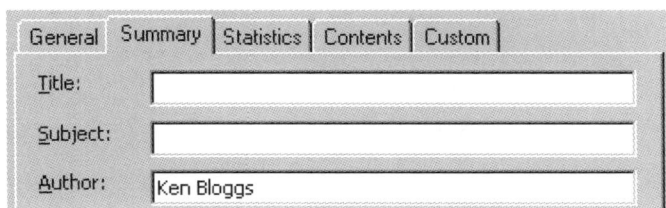

Word displays in this box the user name entered when Windows was installed on your computer. If yours is not the name shown, delete the displayed name, type in your name, and select **OK**.

- Choose **View | Header and Footer**.

- Position the cursor in the header or footer area where you want to insert the author name.

- Choose **Insert | Field** to display the Field dialog box.

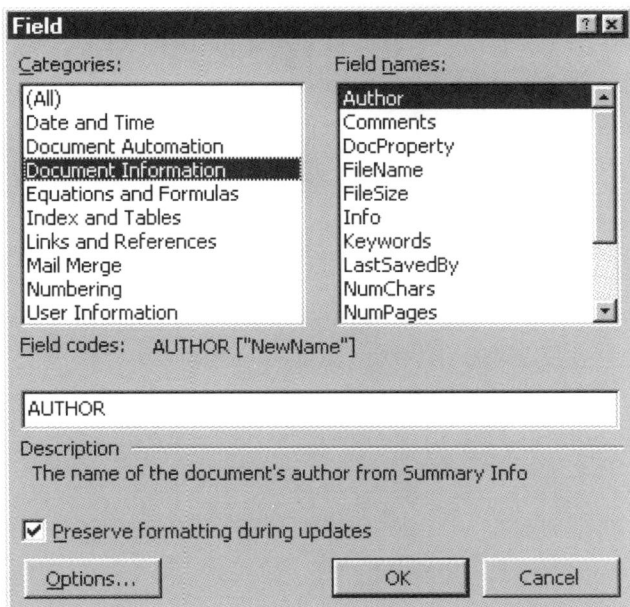

- In the Categories: list, select Document Information. In the Field names: list, select Author. Click **OK**.

## Manual line and page breaks

Pressing Enter at any stage inserts a new paragraph mark, and causes Word to begin a new paragraph. To insert a line break within a paragraph, press Shift+Enter.

John↵
Paul↵
George↵
Ringo¶
¶

*Example of three line breaks*

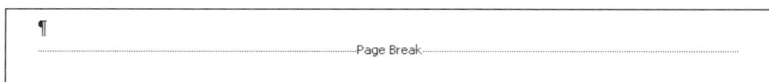

When text fills a page, Word automatically creates another page to hold the additional text.

You can insert a page break manually at any point in a document by pressing Ctrl+Enter. Alternatively, choose the **Insert | Breaks** command, select the Page break option, and click **OK**.

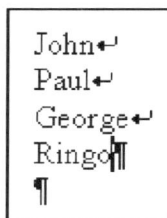

¶
-----------------------------------Page Break-----------------------------------

*Word's manual page break indicator*

## Checking your spelling

How's your spelling? Word can check your spelling and suggest corrections to errors in two ways:

- As you type and edit your document (the automatic option)

- Whenever you choose the **Tools | Spelling and Grammar** command (the on-request option)

To turn automatic spellchecking on or off, select or deselect the Check spelling as you type checkbox on the Spelling & Grammar tab of the Options dialog box. You display this dialog box with the **Tools | Options** command.

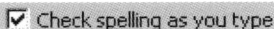

## Spellchecking: the automatic option

As you type and edit, a wavy red line under words indicates possible spelling errors.

To correct an error, right-click the word with a wavy underline, and then select the correction you want from the pop-up menu.

Selecting the last menu option, **Spelling**, displays Word's Spelling and Grammar dialog box.

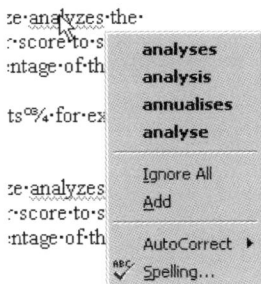

## The spellcheck dialog box

Whether automatic spellchecking is selected or not, you can spellcheck your document at any stage by choosing the **Tools | Spelling and Grammar** command.

If Word's spellchecker finds no errors, it displays a box telling you that the spellcheck is complete.

If Word finds something it does not recognize, it displays the Spelling and Grammar dialog box, and shows the relevant word in red.

Spelling and Grammar: English [U.K.]

Not in Dictionary:

AutoSummarize·analyzes·the·document·and·
assigns·a·score·to·each·sentence.·

Ignore
Ignore All
Add

Suggestions:

analyses
analysis
annualises
analyse

Change
Change All
AutoCorrect

Dictionary language: English (U.K.)
☑ Check grammar

Options...    Undo    Cancel

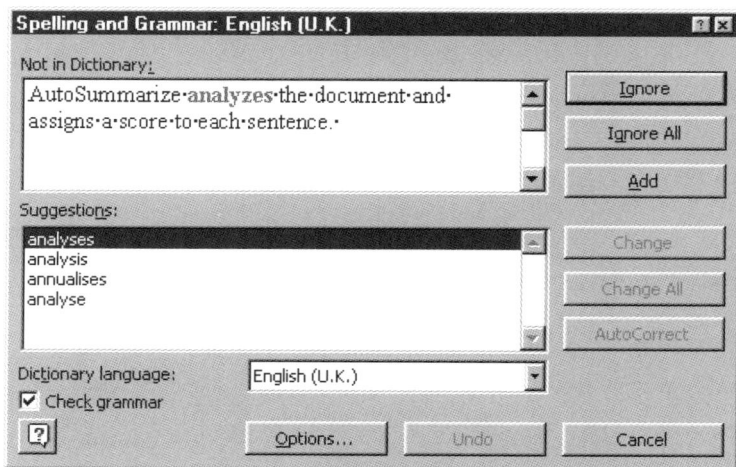

*The Spelling and Grammar dialog box includes a Suggestions area
that offers likely alternatives to queried words. Click on any suggested
word to substitute it for the incorrect one*

Whenever the spellchecker queries a word, your options include:

- **Ignore**: Leave this occurrence of the word unchanged.

- **Ignore All**: Leave this and all other occurrences of the
  word in the document unchanged.

- **Add**: Add the word to the spelling dictionary, so that
  Word will recognize it during future spellchecks of
  any document. Use this option for the names of
  people or places, or abbreviations or acronyms that
  you type regularly.

- **Change**: Correct this occurrence of the word, but
  prompt again on further occurrences.

- **Change All**: Correct this occurrence of the word – and
  all other occurrences, without further prompting.

A word of caution: if the word that you have typed is correctly spelt but inappropriate – for example, 'their' instead of 'there'– your spellchecker will not detect it as an error. Therefore, you should always read over the final version of the document to ensure that it doesn't contain any errors.

### Watch your language

Before spellchecking your documents, choose **Tools | Language | Set Language** to display the current dictionary language.

If it is incorrect (perhaps US English instead of UK English), select your required language and choose **Default**.

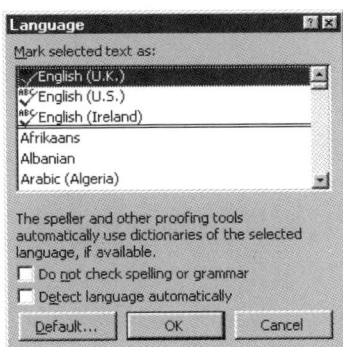

# Checking your grammar

Word can check your grammar and suggest corrections to errors in two ways:

- As you type and edit your document (the automatic option)

- Whenever you choose the **Tools | Spelling and Grammar** command (the on-request option)

To turn automatic grammar-checking on or off, select or deselect the Check grammar as you type or the Check

grammar with spelling checkbox on the Spelling & Grammar
tab of the Options dialog
box. You display this dialog
box with the **Tools |
Options** command.

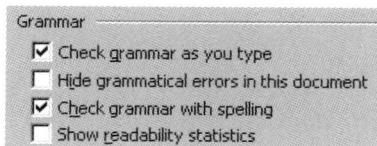

Grammar

☑ Check grammar as you type
☐ Hide grammatical errors in this document
☑ Check grammar with spelling
☐ Show readability statistics

If automatic grammar-
checking is turned on, a wavy green line under words
indicates possible errors. You use Word's grammar-checking
and correction features in the same way as its spellchecker.

# Printing options

Word offers a wide range of printing options. These include
the ability to preview a document on your screen before you
print it, and the choice of printing all of your document, the
current page, selected continuous or non-continuous pages,
or the currently selected text.

### Print preview

This displays each page as it will appear when it is printed on
paper. To preview your document:

- Choose **File | Print Preview** or click
  the Print Preview button on the
  Standard toolbar. Click **Close** to return
  to your document.

*Print Preview
button*

## Print range options

When you choose **File | Print**, you have the following options regarding which pages of your document you may print:

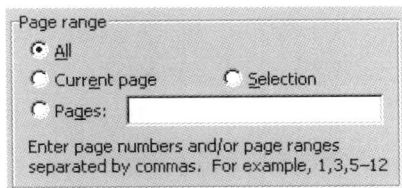

Page range

○ All
○ Current page          ○ Selection
○ Pages: [                    ]

Enter page numbers and/or page ranges separated by commas. For example, 1,3,5–12

- **All**: Prints every page of your document.

- **Current page**: Prints only the currently displayed page.

- **Selection**: Prints only the currently selected text (and/or graphic).

- **Pages**: To print any single page of your document, enter its page number here.

  To print a group of continuous pages, enter the first and last page number of the group, separated by a dash. For example, 2-6 or 12-13.

  To print a non-continuous group of pages, enter their individual page numbers, separated by commas. For example, 3,5,9 or 12,17,34. You can combine continuous with non-continuous page selections.

Other options on the Print dialog box allow you to specify how many copies you want to print of your selected pages, and indicate whether you want to print left or right pages only.

Save and close your long document, and close Microsoft Word.

You have now completed Chapter 3 of the ECDL *Word Processing* module.

# Chapter summary: so now you know

You can increase or decrease Word's default *inter-line* spacing and *inter-paragraph* spacing.

You can highlight the start of each new paragraph by typing an extra paragraph mark (crude, but effective), by increasing inter-paragraph spacing, or by applying a *first-line indent*. The opposite of a first line indent is a *hanging indent*, which is sometimes used for lists.

Word's *find-and-replace* feature enables you quickly to locate a particular piece of text, and replace it with an alternative piece of text. You can also find and replace text with specific formatting, and special characters such as paragraph marks and tabs.

The standard page size is A4, and pages can be oriented as *portrait* or *landscape*. A *margin* is the distance of the text (and graphics) from a particular edge of the page.

*Headers and footers* are small text items that reoccur on every (or every second) page, and typically contain such details as the *document title* and *author name*. Either can also contain the automatically generated *page number*.

Word contains a *spellchecker* and a *grammar-checker*. You can set up these checkers so that they are permanently switched on, or you can run them only as you require.

Word's *print options* include a Print Preview feature and the ability to print one or a range of pages.

# CHAPTER 4

# Tables, tabs and graphics

## In this chapter

On most Word documents, you want text to flow from left to right across the width of the page. Sometimes, however, you may want to create narrow, side-by-side columns of text, numbers, and graphics.

In this chapter you will learn about Word's two options for creating such side-by-side columns: tables and tabs.

You will also discover how to insert and manipulate graphics and AutoShapes in Word.

Finally, you are introduced to hyphenation – a way of splitting long words across lines to improve the appearance of text.

## New skills

At the end of this chapter you should be able to:

- Create and format tables
- Insert and edit tabs
- Paste and insert graphics
- Create AutoShapes
- Move, reshape, and resize graphics and AutoShapes
- Apply automatic and manual hyphenation to text

## New words

At the end of this chapter you should be able to explain the following terms:

- Table
- Tab
- AutoShape
- Hyphenation

# Using tables in Word

A table consists of rectangular cells, arranged in rows and columns. Inside cells, text wraps just as it does on a page. As you type text into a cell, the cell expands vertically to hold each new line.

You can create a new, blank table, and enter text and graphics in its empty cells. Or you can convert existing paragraphs of text to a table.

**Table**

*An array of cells arranged in rows and columns that can hold text and graphics.*

## Exercise 4.1: Creating a new table

In this exercise you create a table, and enter text in it.

1  Open Word and click on the New button on the Standard toolbar to create a new document. Click the Save button to save it. Give your new document a name that you will find easy to remember. If your initials are KB, for example, name it KBtable.doc.

2  Choose **Table | Insert | Table**. In the Insert Table dialog box, select 2 columns and 4 rows, and click **OK**. You can add or remove columns and rows later, as required.

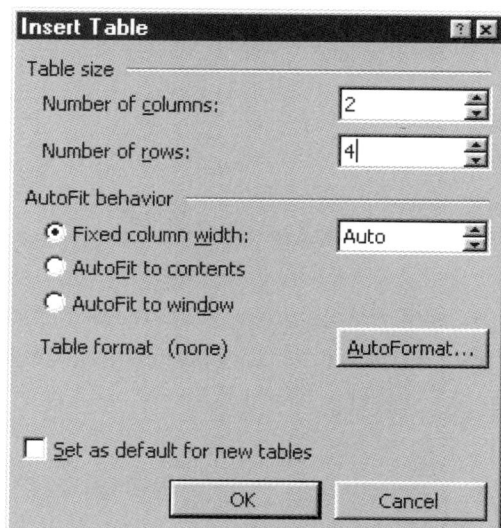

Accept the column width default of Auto. This creates columns of equal size across the width of your page. Word displays a blank table.

3 Click in the top-left cell, and type: Sales Region

4 Press the Tab key. In a table, pressing Tab does not insert a tab stop. Instead, it moves the cursor to the next cell. Shift+Tab moves the cursor back to the previous cell. You can also use the arrow keys or the mouse to move the cursor between different cells. (To insert a tab in a table, press Ctrl+Tab.)

With the cursor in the top-right cell, type the text:
Number of Units Sold

5   Continue moving the cursor and typing text until your
    table looks as shown.

| Sales·Region¤ | Number·of·Units·Sold¤ |
|---|---|
| Europe¤ | 1234¤ |
| Latin·America¤ | 5678¤ |
| China¤ | 4321¤ |

Congratulations. You have created your first table in Word.
Save your table document and leave the Word document open.

# Selecting table cells

You can format and align table text in the same way as text
outside a table. Here are the rules on selecting table text:

*   To select text in a cell, drag the mouse across the text.

*   To select a single
    cell, use the mouse

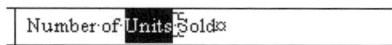

    | Number·of·**Units**·Sold¤ |
    |---|

    to position the cursor over the left edge of the cell, wait
    for the cursor to change to a thick arrow, and then click
    to select the cell.

| 5678¤ | | 5678¤ |
|---|---|---|

*Position cursor ...*                    *... and click*

- To select a row, position the cursor over the left edge of the leftmost cell in the row, wait for the cursor to change to a thick arrow, and then double-click to select the row. (Clicking once selects the leftmost cell only.) Alternatively, click in any cell of the row and choose **Table | Select | Row**.

- To select a column, position the cursor at the top edge of the column, wait for the cursor to change to a thick, downward arrow, and then click to select the column.

| Number of Units Sold¤ | | Number of Units Sold¤ |
| --- | --- | --- |
| 1234¤ | | 1234¤ |
| 5678¤ | | 5678¤ |
| 4321¤ | | 4321¤ |

*Position cursor ...*          *... and click*

Alternatively, click in any cell of the column and choose **Table | Select | Column**.

- To select the entire table, follow these steps:

  - Position the cursor anywhere on the table. Notice that Word displays the table's *move handle* at the top-left of the table.

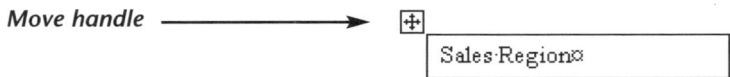

*Move handle* ———————————➤

| Sales Region¤ |
| --- |

  - Click on the move handle to select the entire table.

| Sales Region¤ | Number of Units Sold¤ |
| --- | --- |
| Europe¤ | 1234¤ |
| Latin America¤ | 5678¤ |
| China¤ | 4321¤ |

Alternatively, you can select a table by clicking in any of its cells and choosing **Table | Select | Table**.

# Making changes to a table

Here are the rules for making changes to a table:

* To add a new row, select the row beneath or above the position where you want to insert the new row, and choose **Table | Insert | Rows Above** (or **Rows Below**).

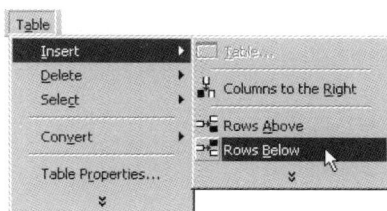

* To add a new column, select the column to the left of where you want to insert the new column, and choose **Table | Insert | Columns to the Right**.

* To delete a row or column, select it, and choose **Table | Delete | Rows** or **Table | Delete | Columns**.

* To merge two or more selected cells from the same row into a single cell, choose **Table | Merge Cells**.

* To split a single, selected cell into two cells on the same row, choose **Table | Split Cells**, enter the required values in the dialog box displayed, and click **OK**.

* To apply borders and shading, select the cells, rows, columns, or entire table, and apply the **Format | Borders and Shading** command.

## Table gridlines

If you turn off table borders, Word displays table non-printing gridlines – thin grey lines that make it easier to see where the rows and columns are in the table. You can turn gridlines off and on with the **Table | Hide/Show Gridlines** command. This command applies to your entire document, and not just a particular table.

## Exercise 4.2: Formatting and changing your table

1  Select the top row of the table you created in Exercise 4.1, choose **Format | Font**, select Arial, 12 pt, Bold, and click **OK**.

2  With the top row still selected, click on the centre-align button on the Formatting toolbar.

| Sales·Region¤ | Number·of·Units·Sold¤ |
|---|---|
| Europe◻ | 1234◻ |

3  Place the cursor in the cell that contains Latin America. Choose **Table | Insert | Rows Above**. Type the following text into the new row.

| South·Africa◻ | 581◻ |
|---|---|

4  Select the top row of the table, and choose **Table | Insert | Rows Above**.

5  With the new, inserted top row still selected, choose **Table | Merge Cells**.

6  Type the following text in the merged row: Sales Figures

7  Select the top, merged row, choose **Format | Font**, select Arial, 14 pt, Bold Italic, and click **OK**.

8  By default, Word places a 1/2 pt black, single solid-line border around each cell. Select the top row, choose **Format | Borders and Shading** and place a double-line border under the first row.

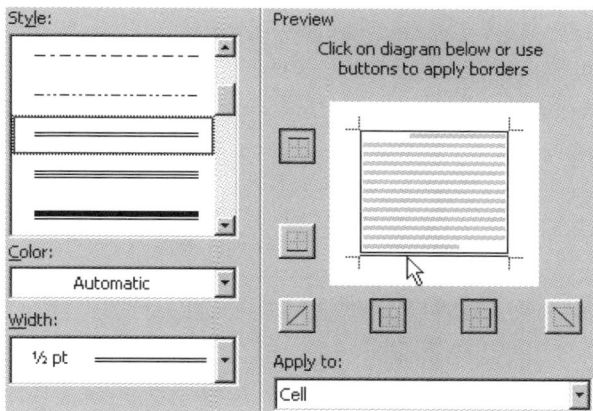

9  Select all rows except the top one, choose **Format | Borders and Shading**, click on the Shading tab, select a 15% grey background, and click **OK**.

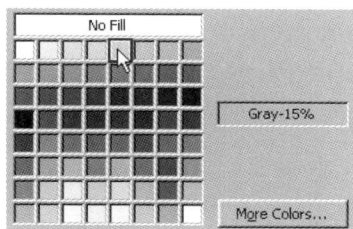

Your table should look as shown. Save your table document again and leave it open.

| *Sales·Figures*¤ | |
|---|---|
| **Sales·Region**¤ | **Number·of·Units·Sold**¤ |
| Europe¤ | 1234¤ |
| Latin·America¤ | 5678¤ |
| South·Africa¤ | 581¤ |
| China¤ | 4321¤ |

# Column width, spacing, and row height

To change the width of a column, use the mouse to position the cursor over the left or right vertical edge of the column. The cursor changes shape. Then drag using the mouse until the column is the width that you require.

As you make a column wider or narrower, Word adjusts the width of the other columns so that the overall table width stays the same. If you hold down the Shift key while dragging a column edge, Word changes the width of the whole table accordingly.

You can change the height of cells in a similar way.

# The Table AutoFormat option

Word's AutoFormat option offers a range of predefined formats for your table, including borders and shading. To apply AutoFormat, select your table and choose **Table | Table AutoFormat**. The Table AutoFormat dialog box offers a preview area where you can view the formatting effects on your table.

*Some examples of Word's AutoFormat options*

Practise by selecting your table and applying a series of AutoFormats. When finished, save and close your table document.

# Introduction to tabs

Old-style typewriters had a key called Tab that, when pressed, changed the position at which the letter keys struck the page and printed text. Typically, there were about ten tab positions – called tab stops – usually about half-an-inch apart.

Pressing the Tab key once advanced the text position to the first tab stop, pressing Tab again moved it to the second tab stop, and so on.

By typing text at the same tab position on successive lines, the typist could create vertical columns of text.

| 1 | 2 | 3 | 4 | 5 | 6 | 7 | 8 | 9 | 10 |
|---|---|---|---|---|---|---|---|---|----|
|  | Cajun·Heat·Fries |  |  |  | £1.45 |  |  |  |  |
|  | Onion·Rings |  |  |  | £1.65 |  |  |  |  |
|  | Bread·Sticks |  |  |  | £1.25 |  |  |  |  |
|  | Fried·Cheese·Ravioli |  |  |  | £2.75 |  |  |  |  |
|  | Primo·Mozzarella·Poppers |  |  |  | £3.25 |  |  |  |  |
|  | Cream·Cheese·Poppers |  |  |  | £3.95 |  |  |  |  |
|  | Breaded·Mushrooms |  |  |  | £2.95 |  |  |  |  |
|  | Breaded·Zucchini·Sticks |  |  |  | £2.75 |  |  |  |  |

The example above shows the second tab stop used to position menu items, and the sixth tab stop used to position menu prices.

As computers and word processing software replaced the typewriter, the idea of tabs continued. Computer keyboards include a Tab key, and Word, like other word-processing applications, offers a tab feature.

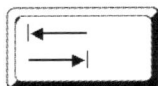

*Tab key*

The effect of using tabs is similar to using tables: text appears in side-by-side columns rather than running continuously from the left to the right margin on the page.

**Tabs**

> *Predefined horizontal locations between the left and right page margins that determine where typed text is positioned. Using tabs on successive lines gives the effect of side-by-side columns of text.*

If you want to position small amounts of text such as the address lines at the top of a letter, tabs are quicker to use than tables. Also, tabs have a feature called *leaders* that tables do not have. These are lines of dots or dashes that can make it easier to read text that is separated into different columns.

# Using tabs in Word

Word automatically positions tab stops at intervals of 1.27 cm (0.5 inch) from left to right. You can see this for yourself by pressing the Tab key repeatedly in a document; each time that you press Tab, Word moves the cursor 1.27 cm to the right.

## Exercise 4.3: Using tab stops

1   Open the letter that you created and saved in Chapter 1.

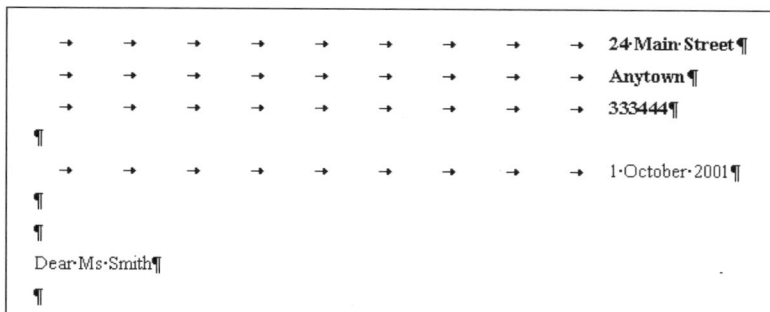

```
    →       →       →       →       →       →       →       →       →    24·Main·Street ¶
    →       →       →       →       →       →       →       →       →    Anytown ¶
    →       →       →       →       →       →       →       →       →    333444¶
¶
    →       →       →       →       →       →       →       →       →    1·October·2001 ¶
¶
¶
Dear·Ms·Smith¶
¶
```

2   Move the cursor to the start of the first line and type: ABC Limited,

3   Move the cursor to the start of the second line and type: Unit 32A,

4   Move the cursor to the start of the third line and type: Smithstown Business Park.

   If your new text pushes any of the sender's address lines to the right or on to the next line, use the Delete key to remove the tab stops from the line until that address line returns to its original position.

5   Your new text picks up the bold formatting of the sender's address. Change its formatting back to normal. Your letter should now look as below.

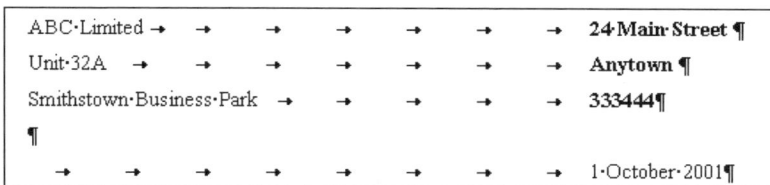

```
ABC·Limited →      →       →       →       →       →       24·Main·Street ¶
Unit·32A    →      →       →       →       →       →       Anytown ¶
Smithstown·Business·Park  →    →       →       →       →    333444¶
¶
    →       →       →       →       →       →       →    1·October·2001¶
```

Save and close your letter document.

In the next exercise you will use Word's tabs to create a restaurant menu.

## Exercise 4.4: Creating a restaurant menu with tabs

1   Open a new document and enter the following text:

> Cajun·Heat·Fries·£1.45·Primo·Mozzarella·Poppers·£3.25¶
>
> Onion·Rings·£1.65·Breaded·Zucchini·Sticks·£2.75¶
>
> Bread·Sticks·£1.25·Fried·Cheese·Ravioli·£2.75¶
>
> Cream·Cheese·Poppers·£3.95·Breaded·Mushrooms·£2.95¶

2   Are Word's tabs measured in centimetres or inches? Find out by choosing **Format | Tabs** to display the Tabs dialog box. Click **OK** to close the box.

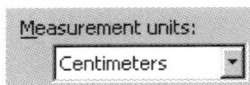

> Measurement units:
>
> Centimeters

If the units are inches, change the tabs to centimetres by choosing **Tools | Options**, selecting the General tab, selecting centimetres, and clicking **OK**.

3   Select all the text in your menu document, and change the font size to 10 points.

4   On the first line of your document, position the cursor at the end of the word Fries, and press Delete to remove the space between Fries and £1.45. Press Tab repeatedly to move the £1.45 rightwards to the 5.08 cm default tab stop.

5   Repeat step 4 for the remaining three lines. Your text should look as below.

```
Cajun·Heat·Fries    →        →    £1.45·Primo·Mozzarella·Poppers·£3.25¶
Onion·Rings →       →        →    £1.65·Breaded·Zucchini·Sticks·£2.75¶
Bread·Sticks →      →        →    £1.25·Fried·Cheese·Ravioli·£2.75¶
Cream·Cheese·Poppers→   →    £3.95·Breaded·Mushrooms·£2.95¶
```

**6**   On the first line, position the cursor after £1.45, and press Delete to remove the space before Primo. Press Tab twice to move the Primo Mozzarella Poppers rightwards to the 7.62 cm default tab stop.

**7**   Repeat step 6 for the remaining three lines.

**8**   On the first line, position the cursor after Poppers, and press Delete to remove the space between Poppers and £3.25. Press Tab repeatedly to move the £3.25 rightwards to the 13.65 cm default tab stop.

**9**   Repeat step 8 for the remaining three lines. Your text should look as below.

```
Cajun·Heat·Fries·  →     →    £1.45→   →    Primo·Mozzarella·Poppers  →   → £3.25¶
Onion·Rings →      →     →    £1.65→   →    Breaded·Zucchini·Sticks   →   → £2.75¶
Bread·Sticks →     →     →    £1.25→   →    Fried·Cheese·Ravioli →    →   → £2.75¶
Cream·Cheese·Poppers→  →  £3.95→  →    Breaded·Mushrooms →   →   → £2.95¶
```

Save your document with a memorable name, and close it. If your initials are KB, for example, call it KBtabsmenu.doc.

# Tab alignment

The tabs you have used so far have all been left-aligned; that is, a tab stop of 5 cm means that the relevant text or number is positioned so that it begins 5 cm in from the left margin. Word offers three other tab alignment options:

- **Centred**: The tabbed text or number is positioned so that its centre is (say) 5 cm from the left margin.

- **Right-aligned**: The tabbed text or number is positioned so that it ends (say) 5 cm from the left margin.

- **Decimal**: If the tabbed item is a number that contains a decimal point, the number is positioned so that the decimal point is (say) 5 cm from the left margin.

If the tabbed item is a number that does not contain a decimal point, or is text, a decimal tab stop has the same effect as a right-aligned tab.

Any tab-stop positions that you insert in a paragraph of a document apply only to that paragraph. This means that different paragraphs of the same document may contain tabs of different types, and tabs positioned at different intervals.

In the next exercise you will practise using all four tab-stop types – left, right, centre, and decimal.

### Exercise 4.5: Using all four tab alignment types

1  Create a new document, and type the text and numbers as shown. Make the text 'Unit Cost' bold.

```
Unit Cost¶
.853 ¶
621¶
45¶
26.82¶
```

2  In turn, select each of the five lines (but not the paragraph mark), and copy and paste it three times to its right. Your document should now look as shown below.

Unit CostUnit CostUnit CostUnit Cost¶
.853.853.853.853¶
621621621621¶
45454545¶
26.8226.8226.8226.82¶

3 Insert four tab stops on each line as shown below. (The tab positions are Word's default ones.)

Unit Cost → Unit Cost → Unit Cost → Unit Cost¶
.853 → .853 → .853 → .853¶
621 → 621 → 621 → 621¶
45 → 45 → 45 → 45¶
26.82 → 26.82 → 26.82 → 26.82¶

4 Select the five lines of text, choose **Format | Tab**, and click **Clear All** to remove all the default tabs.

5 Set the following tab positions and alignments:

| Tab stop position | Alignment |
| --- | --- |
| 2 cm | Left |
| 6 cm | Centre |
| 10 cm | Right |
| 13 cm | Decimal |

In each case, type the tab position, select the alignment, and click **Set**.

6 When finished, click **OK**. Your document should now look as shown.

| → | Unit Cost | → | Unit Cost | → | Unit Cost | → | Unit Cost¶ |
| --- | --- | --- | --- | --- | --- | --- | --- |
| → | .853 | → | .853 | → | .853 | → | .853¶ |
| → | 621 | → | 621 | → | 621 | → | 621¶ |
| → | 45 | → | 45 | → | 45 | → | 45¶ |
| → | 26.82 | → | 26.82 | → | 26.82 | → | 26.82¶ |

Save your document with a memorable name, and close it. If your initials are KB, for example, call it KBunitcost.doc.

# Using tabs with the ruler

You can display and amend Word's default tab stops by choosing **View | Ruler**. The ruler appears along the top of the document window. You can see the default tab stops, indicated by thin vertical lines, at evenly spaced positions along the base of the ruler.

You can change the position of a tab stop by dragging it left or right to a new location on the ruler.

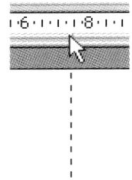

The space between all default tab stops changes proportionately. As you drag a tab stop, Word displays a vertical, dashed line stretching down from the tab ruler to the document itself.

At the left of the ruler you can see the tab alignment button. As you successively click this button, it cycles through the four possible tab alignment values: left-aligned (default), centre-aligned, right-aligned, and decimal point-aligned.

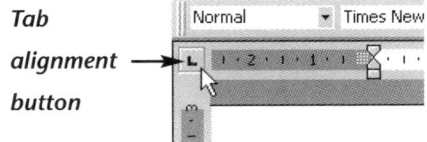

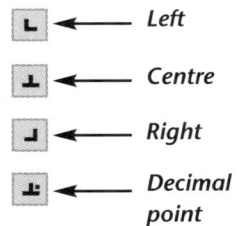

*Tab alignment button*

*Left*

*Centre*

*Right*

*Decimal point*

To add a new tab stop, click the tab button to display the type of tab you want, and then click the ruler where you want to place the tab. To remove a tab stop, click on it and drag it to the right off the ruler.

# Using graphics in Word

You can illustrate your Word documents with graphics of various kinds. For example:

*   Charts (graphs) created in spreadsheet applications such as Excel.

*   Drawings and photographs created or manipulated in graphics applications such as Paint Shop Pro or Adobe Photoshop.

Word contains sixteen categories of standard 'Clip Art' images that you can use and reuse in a wide range of documents. Examples of Clip Art would be Man Answering Phone, Woman Sitting at Desk, Handshake, Sunset, and so on. Clip Art is also available on CD-ROMs and on the internet.

**Clip Art**
> *Standard or stock images that can be used and reused in a wide range of documents.*

# Importing graphics: two options

You have two options for inserting graphics: copy-and-paste, and file insert. Let's look at these two in detail.

## Graphics: copy and paste

This option is possible only if you can open the file
containing the relevant graphic. To do so, you need to have
installed on your computer a software application that can
read that graphic format.

For example, to copy into Word a graphic created in Adobe
Photoshop, you need Adobe Photoshop installed and open
on your computer. Or, failing that, another graphics program
capable of opening Adobe Photoshop files.

When you have the graphic open in your graphics
program, select it (or part of it, as you require), and choose
**Edit | Copy** to copy it to the clipboard. Then, switch to
Word, position the cursor where you want the graphic to
appear in your document, and choose **Edit | Paste**.

## Graphics: file insert

This option enables you to include a graphic in a Word
document – even if you do not have the software package in
which the graphic was created installed on your PC.

Position the cursor where you want the graphic to appear
in your document, and choose **Insert | Picture | From File**.
Locate the relevant graphic – it may be on your hard disk, on
a diskette in the A: drive, or on a CD-ROM – and click **OK** to
insert the image.

To include any of Word's own set of clip art images, choose
the **Insert | Picture | Clip Art** command, click to select the
clip art category, then right-click on the individual image,
and choose **Insert** from the pop-up menu displayed.

# Working with graphics

There are a number of common operations that you can perform on imported graphics, regardless of their type.

## Moving a graphic

To move a graphic, first select it by clicking anywhere inside it. Next, hold down the left mouse button. Word changes the cursor to a cross. Then drag the graphic to its new location.

To move a graphic between documents, use the Cut and Paste commands on the Edit menu.

## Changing the shape and size of a graphic

You can change the shape and size of a graphic by selecting it and clicking on any of its six handles.

Hold down the mouse button and drag the edge of the graphic to change its shape. As you drag the object, Word changes its border to a dashed line.

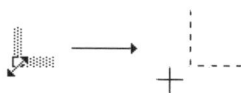

To change a graphic's size but not its shape, hold down the Shift key as you drag with the mouse.

## Exercise 4.6: Inserting a Word clip art image

1  Open the poster document that you created in Chapter 2.

2  Position the cursor at the end of the last line, All Welcome. Press Enter to insert a new paragraph mark.

3  With the cursor positioned at the new paragraph mark, choose **Insert | Picture | Clip Art**, select the **Pictures** tab, scroll down to display the Signs category, and click on it.

Signs

4  Click on the No Smoking symbol, and click **OK**. Word creates a new, second page, and inserts the clip art image on it.

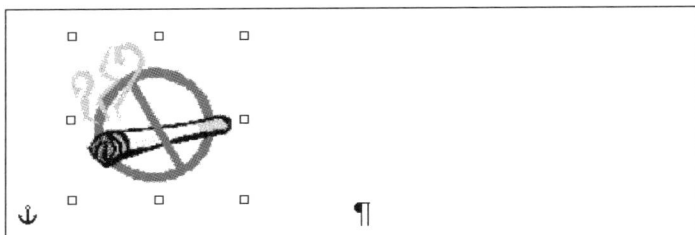

5  Select the graphic, reduce its size by about a half, and drag it until it is under the All Welcome line. Delete the paragraph mark that you typed in step 2. The bottom of your poster should now look as shown. Save your poster.

*All·Welcome¶*

# Inserting AutoShapes

AutoShapes are categories of ready-made shapes that you can insert in your Word documents. They include lines, basic shapes, flowchart elements, stars and banners, and callouts.

When you insert an AutoShape in a
document, you can reposition it, and
change its size and colour, as required.

To select an AutoShape:

| Lines | ▶ |
| Connectors | ▶ |
| Basic Shapes | ▶ |
| Block Arrows | ▶ |
| Flowchart | ▶ |
| Stars and Banners | ▶ |
| Callouts | ▶ |
| Action Buttons | ▶ |

AutoShapes ▾

- Display Word's Drawing
  toolbar by choosing **View |
  Toolbars | Drawing**.

- Click the AutoShapes button on
  the Drawing toolbar.

You can then choose from the options offered by the
pop-up menu.

**AutoShapes**

> *Categories of ready-made shapes, including lines,
> geometric shapes, and flowchart elements, which you can
> use in your Word documents.*

When you right-click on an AutoShape, Word offers a
number of options including:

- **Add Text:** This enables you to
  type characters inside the circle,
  square, oval, or other
  AutoShape. You can also paste
  text from the clipboard into an
  AutoShape.

| Cut |
| Copy |
| Paste |
| Add Text |
| Grouping ▶ |
| Order ▶ |
| Set AutoShape Defaults |
| Format AutoShape... |
| Hyperlink... |

- **Format AutoShape**: This
  enables you to change the
  border (edge) and fill
  (background) colours of the AutoShape.

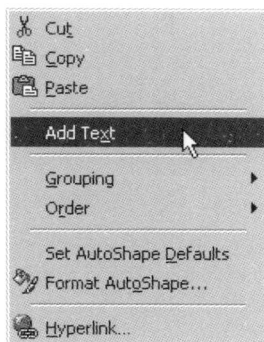

You can move and resize AutoShapes in the same way that you can graphics.

Exercise 4.7 provides examples of creating AutoShapes and applying AutoShape features.

## Exercise 4.7: Working with AutoShapes

1   If your poster document is not open after Exercise 4.6, open it now.

2   Select the text Admission Free (but not its accompanying paragraph mark).

**Admission·Free**¶

3   Cut the selected text from the poster to the clipboard.

4   With the cursor positioned at the paragraph mark of the cut text, press Enter to insert a second paragraph mark.

5   With the cursor positioned at the first of the two paragraph marks, choose **View | Toolbars**, and select the Drawing toolbar option.

> Control Toolbox
> Database
> ✓ Drawing
> Forms

6   Click the AutoShapes button on the Drawing toolbar. From the pop-up menu displayed, select **Basic Shapes**. Finally, select the Rounded Rectangle AutoShape.

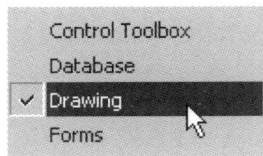

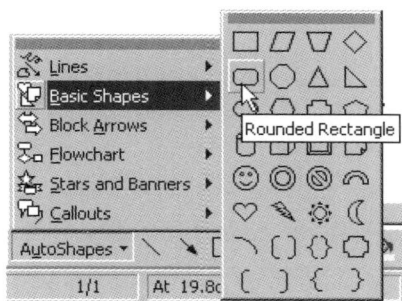

**7**  Draw the AutoShape so that it is big enough to hold the
text in the clipboard. Position it so that it is centred
between the left and right page margins.

Sunday, 17 October¶

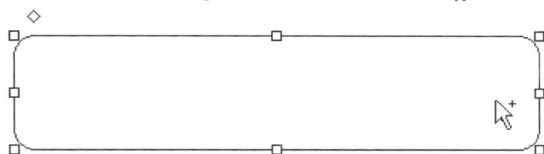

*All Welcome*¶

**8**  Right-click on the AutoShape, choose **Add Text**, and paste
the text from the clipboard to the AutoShape. Select the
pasted text, and choose the Center button to centre it
within the AutoShape. Make the text Arial, 20 point, Bold.

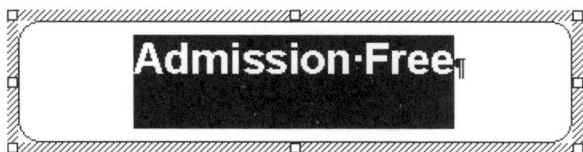

**9**  Click any edge of the AutoShape to select it, right-click to
display the pop-up menu, and choose **Format AutoShape**.

On the Colours and Lines tab, select a Fill colour of Yellow. Also, change the Line Weight to 1.5 pt.

10  Select the text within the AutoShape, and, using the **Format | Paragraph** command, change the Spacing Before until the text is centred vertically between the top and bottom edges of the AutoShape. The new poster layout should now look as shown.

**When:¶**
2pm,·¶
Sunday,·17·October¶

**Admission·Free¶**

*All·Welcome*¶

Save and close your poster document.

# Hyphenating justified text

In Chapter 2 you learned about an alignment option called justification, whereby text is aligned against both the left and right margins. Justification is typically used for the narrow columns of text found in newspapers and magazines.

Justified columns can contain a lot of white (that is, blank) space, because Word spreads out the text in order to align it with both margins simultaneously. This is particularly true when the text contains a lot of long words.

Hyphenation – the process of breaking up long words and splitting them across two lines – gives justified text a more professional appearance. Consider the following two examples:

| |
|---|
| Word spreads out the text in order to align it with both           m argins simultaneously. This is particularly true when the text contains a lot of long words. |

*Hyphenation off*

| |
|---|
| Word spreads out the text in order to align it with both margins simultane-ously. This is particularly true when the text con-tains a lot of long words. |

*Hyphenation on*

Word applies two rules when hyphenating text: certain words are never hyphenated, and words that are hyphenated are split only in certain places. Word allows you to hyphenate both justified and unjustified text.

### Hyphenation

*The process of splitting a long word across two successive lines to avoid unsightly amounts of white space. Used mostly in narrow, justified columns of text.*

You can hyphenate text in two ways: automatically or manually.

# Automatic hyphenation

Word can hyphenate your document automatically as

☑ Automatically hyphenate document

you type. To use this option, choose **Tools | Language | Hyphenation**, select the Automatically hyphenate document checkbox, and click **OK**.

### Automatic hyphenation options

If you select automatic hyphenation, Word offers you a number of options that let you control how it applies hyphenation to your document.

- **Text in Capitals**: Typically, only headings are in capitals, so you can decide to turn automatic hyphenation off for capitalized text.

- **Hyphenation Zone**: The amount of space that Word leaves between the end of the last word in a line and the right margin. It applies only to unjustified text. Make the zone wider to reduce the number of hyphens, or narrower to reduce the raggedness of the right margin.

- **Consecutive Hyphens**: The number of consecutive lines that Word hyphenates.

# Manual hyphenation

If you don't want Word to insert hyphens in your text automatically, ensure that the Automatically hyphenate document checkbox is deselected.

The better option is to turn automatic hyphenation off, and run manual hyphenation after you have finished writing and editing, and adding and removing text.

### Running manual hyphenation

To hyphenate your document (or a selected part of it) manually, choose **Tools | Language | Hyphenation** and click **Manual**.

Word scans through your text, and when it finds a word it thinks it should hyphenate, it displays a dialog box similar to the one below.

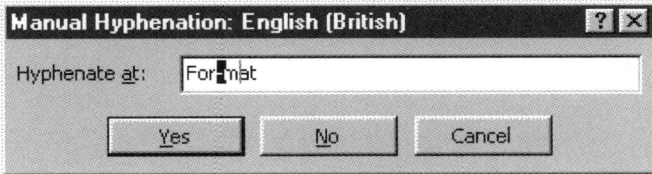

```
┌─────────────────────────────────────────────────────────┐
│ Manual Hyphenation: English (British)            [?][X]   │
│                                                           │
│ Hyphenate at:   ┌─────────────────────────────────────┐  │
│                 │ For│mat                              │  │
│                 └─────────────────────────────────────┘  │
│                                                           │
│        ┌──────────┐  ┌──────────┐  ┌──────────┐          │
│        │   Yes    │  │   No     │  │  Cancel  │          │
│        └──────────┘  └──────────┘  └──────────┘          │
└─────────────────────────────────────────────────────────┘
```

Click **Yes** if you want Word to insert a hyphen in the suggested location. If you prefer Word to insert the hyphen at a different location, move the cursor to that location, and then click **Yes**. Alternatively, click **No** to leave the word unbroken.

You can close any open documents and exit Microsoft Word. You have now completed Chapter 4 of the ECDL *Word Processing* module.

# Chapter summary: so now you know

A Word *table* consists of rectangular cells arranged in rows and columns. As required, you can insert and delete rows and columns in a table, split a single cell into two cells, or merge multiple cells into a single cell.

You can also change row and column height and width, apply formatting, and add borders and shading. Word's *AutoFormat* option provides a quick way to improve the appearance of any table.

*Tabs* are predefined horizontal locations that, when used on successive lines, give the appearance of columns. *Tab leaders* are dashed, dotted, or continuous lines that draw the reader's eye from one tabbed column to the next.

You can add *graphics* to a Word document in two ways: by using copy and paste, or by inserting the graphic as a file. You can move, reposition, resize, or change the shape of any graphic.

*AutoShapes* are ready-made shapes that you can insert in your Word documents. They include lines, basic shapes, flowchart elements, stars and banners, and callouts (identifying labels). You can manipulate AutoShapes in a similar way to graphics.

You can use Word's *hyphenation* feature to remove unsightly amounts of white space by splitting long words across successive lines. Hyphenation is applied mostly to narrow columns of justified text.

# CHAPTER 5

# Mail merge and templates

## In this chapter

Bulk mail is the name given to mass-produced letters that contain individual names and addresses (as in 'Dear Ms Murray') but have the same basic text (as in 'Allow us to introduce our Spring Promotion...'). A more commonly used term might be junk mail.

How is it done? Each letter is basically the same, but clearly no one letter is just a copy of another, as each is slightly different. Read this chapter to find out.

Hint: each letter is the result of combining ('merging') two separate files: the form letter, which contains the basic text; and the data source, which holds a list of names, addresses, and other details.

Also in this chapter you will learn about templates and styles. These are quick, convenient ways to create documents that can contain ready-made text, images, formatting, and page settings.

## New skills

At the end of this chapter you should be able to:
- Create the two components of a merged letter: the form letter and the data source
- Select the appropriate merge fields and insert them in a form letter
- Merge a form letter with a data source to produce a mail merge
- Explain the two possible roles of a Word template: document model, and interface controller
- Choose an appropriate Word template for a document type
- Explain the relationship between styles and templates, and apply styles to selected text
- Attach a different template to a document, and create a new template
- Apply Word's document views – normal, print layout, and outline

## New words

At the end of this chapter you should be able to explain the following terms:
- Form letter
- Template
- Data source
- Style
- Merge field
- Normal view
- Print layout view
- Outline view

# Mail merge: the components

Think of a mail merge as composed of two components: a form letter and a data source. And think of merge fields as the glue that binds the two together. Read on to discover what these three terms mean.

## Form letter

The form letter holds the text that remains the same in every letter – plus punctuation, spaces, and perhaps graphics.

You never type the names or addresses in the form letter, because these will be different on each copy of the final, merged letter.

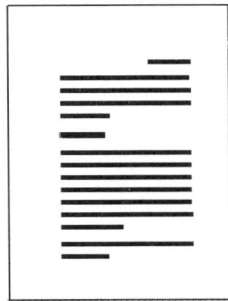

**Form letter**

*A Word document containing information (text, spaces, punctuation, and graphics) that remains the same in each copy of the merged letter.*

## Data source

The data source holds the information that changes for each copy of the final, merged letter – the names and addresses of the people that you want to send the merged letters to.

You can create a data source in Word, or in a spreadsheet (such as Excel) or database (such as Access). Whichever file type you use, its contents must be arranged in a table. Along the top row must be the titles identifying the information categories in the columns underneath, such as Title or Last Name.

**Data source**

*A file containing information (such as names and addresses) that will be different in each merged copy of the final letter.*

## Merge fields

The merge fields are special instructions that you insert in your form letter. They tell Word which details you want to merge from your data source, and where Word is to position them in your merged letter.

Merge fields have names such as Job Title, First Name, and Town. When you merge the

«FirstName»¶

«Title»·«LastName»,¶

«Company».¶

*Merge fields are enclosed within double angle brackets. In the merged letter, Word replaces the merge fields with the associated details from the data source.*

form letter and the data source, Word replaces the merge fields in the form letter with the associated details from the data source. For example, Word might replace the merge field called Town with Bristol, Carlisle, or Derby on different copies of the merged letter.

### Merge field

*An instruction to Word to insert a particular type of information, such as job title or a line of an address, in a specified location on the form letter.*

# Mail merge: the procedure

You can think of a mail merge as a five-step process. Steps one and two are about preparing the ingredients: the form letter and the data source.

In step three, you make the connection between the two by inserting the merge fields in your form letter – one merge field for every item of information that you want to merge to the form letter from the data source.

Step four is optional, but recommended. Before you produce your merged letters, take a preview of the first one or two to check that the merge worked successfully.

Finally, in step five, print your merged letters.

### One: prepare your form letter

A form letter is simply a Word document. Using the **Tools | Mail Merge** command, you can do one of the following:

- Create a new letter especially for the merge operation.

- Select a letter you have already typed as the form letter.

Exercises 5.1 and 5.2 show you how to perform these steps.

## Two: prepare your data source

Again, using the **Tools | Mail Merge** command, you can do one of the following:

- Create a new Word file and enter the names, addresses, and other details of the people you plan to send the merged letter to

  –or–

- Select a file created in another software application.

You will learn how to create a Word data source in Exercise 5.3.

## Three: insert merge fields in your form letter

When you open your form letter on screen, Word displays a special Mail Merge toolbar. One of its buttons is called Insert Merge Field. This is the one you use to select and then position the merge fields in your form letter. Exercise 5.4 shows you how to insert the merge field codes.

| Insert Merge Field ▾ | Insert Word Field ▾ | 🔤 | ◄ | ◄ | 1 | ► | ►| | 🖳 | 🖎 | 🖳 🖳 🖳 | 🙀 | 🖃 |

*Click here to select
and insert merge
fields in your
form letter*

*Click here to preview
the first few merged
letters, before
printing*

*Click here to perform
the complete merge
operation*

## Four: preview your merged letters

Before you produce your (perhaps hundreds or thousands!) of merged letters, click on the toolbar's View Merged Data button to preview the first one or two merged letters.

You will learn how to preview your merged letters in Exercise 5.5.

## Five: print your merged letters

If you are happy with the preview, click on the Mail Merge button to perform the complete merge operation. Select the **Merge to Printer** option to output copies of your merged letters.

Merge to:

Printer

You will learn how to print your merged letters in Exercise 5.6.

Word gives you the option of saving all the merged letters in a single file. You don't need to do this, because you can quickly recreate them at any stage by rerunning the merge operation.

# Your mail merge exercises

Exercises 5.1 to 5.6 take you, step-by-step, through a complete, worked example of a mail merge operation.

For these exercises, we will assume that the merged letters are produced on pre-printed paper that already contains the sender's name and address. Only the recipients' names and addresses need therefore be inserted.

## Exercise 5.1: Using an existing document as a form letter

Do you still have the letter you saved from Exercise 4.3? If so, this exercise shows you how to use that text as a basis for your form letter.

If not, proceed to Exercise 5.2 to create a new form letter from scratch.

1 Open the file that you saved in Exercise 4.3 of Chapter 4.

2 Remove the recipient's name and address from the top left of the letter, and remove the sender's address from the top right. Also delete the 'Ms Smith' after the word 'Dear'.

3 At the top left, type 'To:' and press Tab. Insert three new lines, each with a tab stop, under the 'To:'. Your letter should look like that shown.

```
To: →  ¶
    →  ¶
    →  ¶
    →  ¶
    →    →    →    →    →    →    →    →   1·October·2001¶
Dear·¶
¶
I·am·writing·to·you·in·relation·to·our·annual·Sale·of·Work·which·will·take·place·in·our·local·
Scout·Hall·on·17·October.¶
¶
In·previous·years·your·company·was·kind·enough·to·donate·a·prize·for·our·wheel·of·fortune.¶
¶
Could·we·ask·you·to·be·as·generous·again·this·year?¶
¶
_____¶
Ken·Bloggs¶
```

4  Choose **Tools | Mail Merge** to display the Mail Merge Helper dialog box.

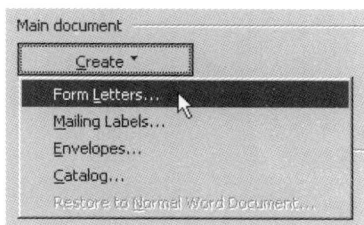

5  In the Main document area, click the **Create** button to display a drop-down list of options.

From this list, select the option named **Form Letters**.

6  On the next dialog box displayed, click the **Active Window** button.

7  Word next displays a dialog box that asks you to select or create a data source. Proceed to Exercise 5.3.

## Exercise 5.2: Creating a new form letter

Follow this exercise to create a new form letter for a mail merge operation.

1  Choose **Tools | Mail Merge** to display the Mail Merge Helper dialog box.

2  In the Main Document area, choose the **Create** button to display a drop-down list of options.

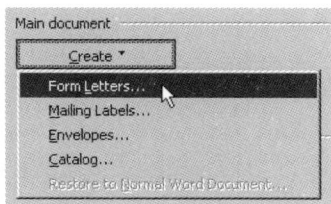

From this list, select the option called **Form Letters**.

3  On the next dialog box displayed, click the **New Main Document** button.

4   Word opens a new document on your screen for you to enter the text of your form letter, and displays an Edit button to the right of the Create button in the Main Document area.

Click the Edit button, then click the document name button that appears beneath it, and type the text as shown in Exercise 5.1.

5   Click the File Save button (or press Ctrl+s) and give your new document a name that you will find easy to remember. If your initials are KB, for example, name it KBformlet.doc.

Proceed to Exercise 5.3.

### Exercise 5.3: Creating a data source

In this exercise you create your data source to contain the names, addresses and other information that will vary on each copy of the final, merged letter.

Do not begin this exercise until you have completed either Exercise 5.1 or 5.2.

1   If the Mail Merge Helper dialog box is not already open, choose **Tools | Mail Merge** to display it.

2   In the Data Source area, choose the **Get Data** button to display a drop-down list of options.

From this list, select the option called **Create Data Source**.

3   Word now displays the Create Data Source dialog box.

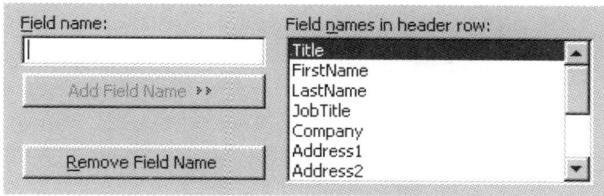

| Field name: | Field names in header row: |
|---|---|
| [          ] | Title |
| Add Field Name >> | FirstName |
| | LastName |
| | JobTitle |
| | Company |
| Remove Field Name | Address1 |
| | Address2 |

4   In the case of each of the following merge fields, click the field name in the list displayed then click the **Remove Field Name** button to delete them: JobTitle, City, State, Postal Code, Country, Home Phone, and Work Phone.

5   You now have all the merge fields that you need. Click **OK**.

6   Word next asks you to name and save your Data Source file. If your initials are KB, for example, name it KBDataSource and click **Save**.

7   You are now shown the dialog box below. Click **Edit Data Source**.

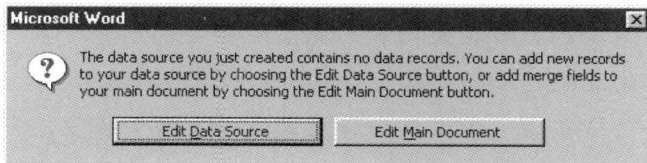

| Microsoft Word | ✕ |
|---|---|
| ? | The data source you just created contains no data records. You can add new records to your data source by choosing the Edit Data Source button, or add merge fields to your main document by choosing the Edit Main Document button. |
| | Edit Data Source      Edit Main Document |

8   Word displays a Data Form dialog box. Enter the information as shown and click **Add New**.

9   Enter a second set of details in the Data Form dialog box as shown below. Click **Add New** and then click **OK**.

You have now created a Data Source with two records – enough for this exercise. But you can easily imagine a Data Source with hundreds or thousands of records, each record holding the name, address, and other information regarding a particular person or organization.

### Viewing your Word data source

You can open, view, and edit your data source file just as you can any other Word document. Open the data source you created in Exercise 5.3. It should look as follows:

| Title¤ | FirstName¤ | LastName¤ | Company¤ | Address1¤ | Address2¤ | ¤ |
|---|---|---|---|---|---|---|
| Dr¤ | Mary¤ | Mulligan¤ | Clamour·Chemicals¤ | Unit·46¤ | New·Business·Park¤ | ¤ |
| Ms¤ | Liz¤ | Walsh¤ | Atcatin·Printers¤ | The·New·Mall¤ | Main·Street¤ | ¤ |

**Header Row** ——→

**Record 1** ——→

**Record 2** ——→

¶

You can see a header row containing the merge field names such as FirstName and LastName. And under the header row are the records themselves, each in a row of its own.

### Using non-Word data sources

Does your data source have to be a Word document? No. You can also use files created in a spreadsheet such as Excel or a database such as Access. The only requirement is that the information is arranged in the same type of table format: a single, top row of merge field titles, followed by other rows holding individual records.

# Inserting merge codes in your form letter

Before you move on to the mail merge operation, you need to perform one more step. You must insert the merge field codes in your form letter. Exercise 5.4 shows you how.

### Exercise 5.4: Inserting the merge field codes

1   Open your form letter document.

2   For each merge field:

   • Place the cursor in the appropriate position in your form letter

- Click the Insert Merge Field button on the Mail Merge Toolbar, which Word now displays at the top of your screen.

- Click the relevant field title from the drop-down list.

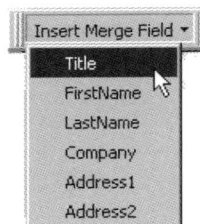

| Insert Merge Field ▾ |
|---|
| Title |
| FirstName |
| LastName |
| Company |
| Address1 |
| Address2 |

Continue until your form letter looks like the sample shown.

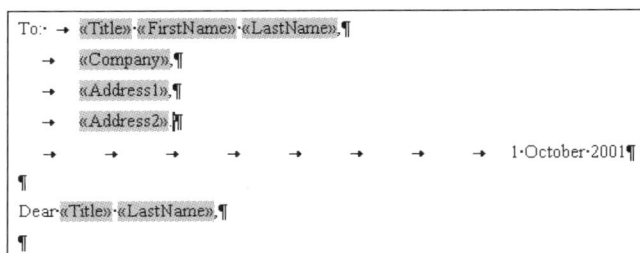

To:·  →  «Title»·«FirstName»·«LastName»,¶
  →  «Company»,¶
  →  «Address1»,¶
  →  «Address2»,¶
  →    →    →    →    →    →    →    →   1·October·2001¶
¶
Dear·«Title»·«LastName»,¶
¶

Do not forget to type spaces between merge fields just as you would between ordinary text. Also, type commas or full stops at the end of lines.

Save and name your form letter when finished.

Now everything is in place for the mail merge operation.

### Exercise 5.5: Previewing the mail merge

1 If your form letter is not already open, open it now and make it the active window.

2 Click the View Merged Data button on the Mail Merge toolbar. Word displays the first merged letter. It should look as shown below.

《 》
ABC

*View Merged*
*Data button*

---

To: → Dr·Mary·Mulligan,¶
    → Clamour·Chemicals,¶
    → Unit·46,¶
    → New·Business·Park.¶
    →  →  →  →  →  →  →    → 1·October·2000¶
¶
Dear·Dr·Mulligan,¶
¶

---

**3** You can view the second merged letter by clicking the forward arrow button on the Mail Merge toolbar.

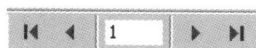

*Arrow buttons*

You are now ready to perform the mail merge.

## Exercise 5.6: Performing the mail merge

**1** If your form letter is not already open, open it now and make it the active window.

**2** Click the Mail Merge button on the Mail Merge toolbar to display the Merge dialog box. Select the options as shown below and click **Merge**.

*Mail Merge button*

Merge

Merge to:
Printer

Setup...

Records to be merged
● All ○ From: [    ] To: [    ]

When merging records
● Don't print blank lines when data fields are empty.
○ Print blank lines when data fields are empty.

No query options have been set.

Merge
Close
Check Errors...
Query Options...

3  Word now displays the Printer dialog box. Click **OK**.
Your form letter and the two records from the data
source are now merged to the printer.

Congratulations! You have performed your first mail merge
in Word.

# Merging addresses to labels

You can use Word's mail merge features to print a list of names
and addresses (or any other list of structured information) on
adhesive labels. Exercise 5.7 shows you how.

### Exercise 5.7: Merging to address labels

1  Open a new Word document.

2  Chose **Tools | Mail Merge**.

3  Click **Create**, select the
Mailing Labels option, and
then click the **Active
Window** button.

Main document
Create ▾
Form Letters...
Mailing Labels...
Envelopes...
Catalog...
Restore to Normal Word Document...

4  Click **Get Data** to select the source of the names and
address that you want to use. Word offers three options:

• **Create Data Source**: Select this to enter the name
and address information in Word.

• **Open Data Source**: Select this to use a list of names
and addresses that is contained in an existing Word
document (or in a spreadsheet, a database, or
other list).

- **Use Address Book**: Select this to use names and addresses from an electronic address book such as that contained in Outlook Express.

  For this exercise, choose the **Open Data Source** option, and select the Word document that you created as a data source in Exercise 5.3.

5 Click **Set Up Main Document**.

  In the Label Options dialog box, select the type of printer and the type of labels you want to use, and click **OK**.

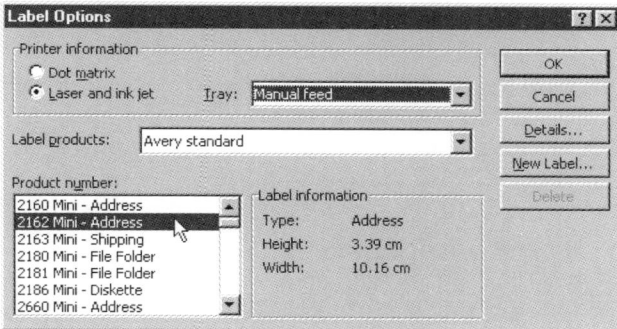

| Label Options | | ? X |
|---|---|---|
| **Printer information** | | OK |
| ○ Dot matrix | | Cancel |
| ● Laser and ink jet  Tray: [Manual feed ▾] | | Details... |
| Label products: [Avery standard ▾] | | New Label... |
| **Product number:** | **Label information** | Delete |
| 2160 Mini - Address | | |
| 2162 Mini - Address | Type: Address | |
| 2163 Mini - Shipping | Height: 3.39 cm | |
| 2180 Mini - File Folder | Width: 10.16 cm | |
| 2181 Mini - File Folder | | |
| 2186 Mini - Diskette | | |
| 2660 Mini - Address | | |

6 In the Create Labels dialog box, insert the merge fields for the address information.

7 In the Mail Merge Helper dialog box, click **Merge**.

8 In the Merge to: box, click **Printer** to merge to the selected printer.

Well done! That completes your mail merge exercises.

# Word templates

Microsoft Word is made up of three components: the Word software application itself, the document files that Word produces, and a third component, which you now meet for the first time: templates.

- **Word application**: This provides the standard Word menus, commands, and toolbars – the things you use to create and work with documents.

- **Document files**: Look in any of these and you will find the text, graphics, formatting, and settings such as margins and page layout for that particular document.

- **Word templates**: These have two main purposes. They can:

  - Provide a model for creating documents

  - Control Word's interface: the menus, commands, and toolbars available to the user.

### A template as a document model

A template can act as a document model by storing:

- Built-in text and graphics such as your company's name and logo. These are sometimes called 'boilerplate' text and graphics.

- Preset formatting (such as font settings) and text positioning (such as alignment, indents, tab stops, and inter-line and inter-paragraph spacing settings).

- Preset page settings (such as margins and page orientation).

For example, you could save everyone in your organization time by creating a memo template that contained preset margins, the company logo, and text for standard headings such as 'Memo', 'To:', and 'From:'. With much of the formatting and typing already done, users simply fill in the additional text.

### A template as an interface controller

A template can also store customized Word commands, menus and toolbar settings. This allows managers to remove unused and unnecessary features, and adapt Word to meet the needs of different levels of users.

For example, you could create a template that helped new Word users by displaying a customized toolbar with buttons and menus to lead them through everyday tasks.

# Templates and documents

Whether you realised it or not, every new Word document that you have created has been based on a template.

A single template can provide the basis for lots of documents. But each document can be based on only a single template at a time.

A template, like a document, is a Word file. Whereas document file names end in .doc, template file names end in .dot.

### The Normal.dot template

Unless you choose otherwise, every new Word document you create is based on a template called Normal.dot.

In addition to this standard, all-purpose template, Word provides templates for specific document types such as letters, memos, and reports.

#### Word template

*A file that can contain ready-made text, formatting and page settings, and interface controls. Every Word document is based on, and takes its characteristics from, a template of one kind or another.*

### Templates and new documents

In Chapter 1, you learned two ways to create a new document:

- Clicking on the New button on the Standard toolbar

- Choosing the **File | New** command.

*New button*

If you click the New button, Word automatically bases your new document on the Normal.dot template.

Choose **File | New**, however, and Word presents you with a wide range of templates to choose from. You will find the various templates on different tabs of the New dialog box.

### Exercise 5.8: Previewing Word's templates

1    Choose **File | New** to display the New dialog box.

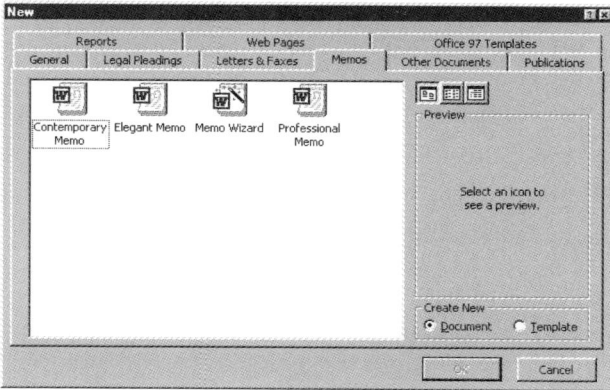

2   Click on the various tabs to view the available templates.

3   Click on the various templates to view a miniature of them in the Preview area on the right of the dialog box.

# Templates and styles

At the top-left of the Standard toolbar is a drop-down list box containing items called Normal, Heading 1, Heading 2, and so on. These items are called styles.

For ECDL, you need know only four things about styles:

- A style is a bundle of formatting and text positioning settings.

- You apply a style by first positioning the cursor in the text, and then clicking on that style from the drop-down list.

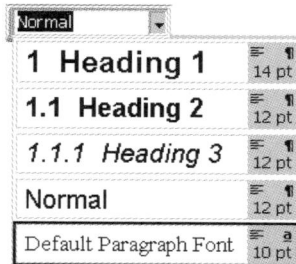

*Style drop-down list box*

- Unless you choose otherwise, Word applies the style called Normal to all text you type in a document.

- Styles are linked to templates. For example, in one template the style called Heading 3 might be centre-aligned, Times, 10 point, italic. In another, Heading 3 might be left-aligned, Arial, 12 point, bold.

## Exercise 5.9: Applying a style to text

In this exercise you will open a document that you previously created and saved, and apply a style to its headings.

1  Open the document that you saved in Exercise 3.9 of Chapter 3.

2  Choose **Edit | Replace**, and on the **Replace** tab, type the text Heading One in both the Find what: and Replace with: boxes.

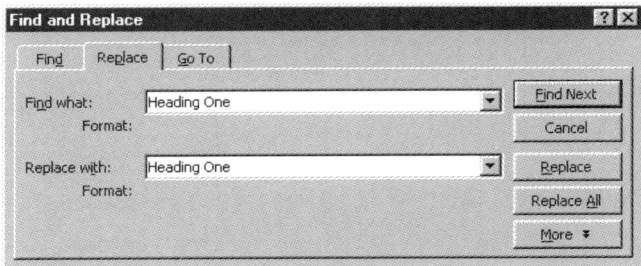

3  With the cursor in the Replace with: box, click the **More** button. Next, click the **No Formatting** button to remove the formatting left over from previous exercises.

4  Select the option **Style** from the pop-up menu, and then select the style Heading 1 from the list displayed. Click **OK**.

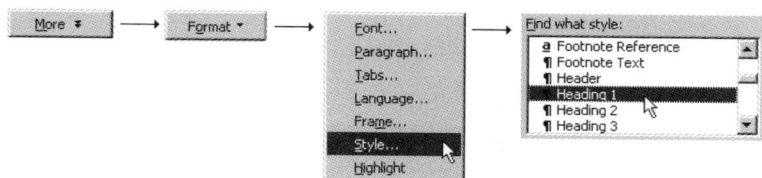

5   You are returned to the Find and Replace dialog box.
Click **Replace All**.

Word now applies the style called Heading 1 to all the
headings in your document. Unless you have at some
stage changed the Heading 1 style that comes with
Normal.dot, the Heading 1 font should be Arial 14
point, bold. Save the document.

## Why use styles?

Using styles to control the appearance of a document has
three advantages:

*   You can apply a bundle of formatting and text
    positioning settings to a piece of selected text in a
    single, quick operation.

*   By changing the settings of a particular style, Word can
    automatically apply your new settings to all occurrences
    of text in that style throughout the entire document.

    For example, by changing the Heading 1 style from bold
    to italic, all text with the Heading 1 style changes from
    bold to italic. This is much faster than individually
    selecting and then changing every heading.

*   If you change the template on which a document is
    based, the document takes its style settings from the
    new template.

You can therefore change the entire appearance of a document by linking it with a different template. Exercise 5.10 illustrates this point.

### Style

*A collection of formatting and positioning settings that you can apply to selected text in a single operation. Styles are linked to templates, and can have different settings in different templates.*

## Exercise 5.10: Attaching a different template to a document

1   If the document you worked with in Exercise 5.9 is not already open, open it now. Select all the text in the document, and chose **Edit | Copy** (or Ctrl+c). You can now close that document.

2   Choose **File | New** to display the New dialog box. Click the **Reports** tab, and then click the template called Professional Report.dot. Finally, click **OK**.

Professional Report

3   Word opens a new document that is based on Professional Report.dot.

    This contains instructions which you can ignore. Hold down the Ctrl key and click in the left margin to select everything in the new document, and then press Delete to delete the new document's contents.

4   Choose **Edit | Paste** (or press Ctrl+v) to paste the text copied from your document into the new document. Save and name your new document.

---

**Heading·One¶**

How·does·AutoSummarize·determine·what·the·key·points·are?·AutoSummarize· analyzes·the·document·and·assigns·a·score·to·each·sentence.·(For·example,·it·gives· a·higher·score·to·sentences·that·contain·words·used·frequently·in·the·document.)·You· then·choose·a·percentage·of·the·highest·scoring·sentences·to·display·in·the·summary.¶
Keep·in·mind·that·AutoSummarize·works·best·on·well-structured·documents·- for·example,·reports,·articles,·and·scientific·papers.¶

---

Notice how all text in your document with the Normal and Heading 1 styles changes in appearance. This is because such text is now taking its settings from the Professional Report.dot template – and not from the Normal.dot template on which the document was originally based.

You can now close the document.

# Creating a new template

Word offers a number of ways of creating a new template. Here is the easiest way:

- Create a document that has the features you want in your template – some boilerplate text, perhaps, or a particular margin setting.

- With the document open on your screen, save it, not as a document, but as a template.

In future, whenever you use the **File | New** command to create a document, your new template appears as an option on the General tab of the New dialog box.

Exercise 5.11 takes you through an example of this procedure.

## Exercise 5.11: Creating a new template

1 Create a new document and enter the following:

Bloggs·Limited·Monthly·Expenses·Report¶

| Item | Amount |
|------|--------|
|      |        |
|      |        |
|      |        |
|      |        |
|      |        |
|      |        |
|      |        |
|      |        |
|      |        |
|      |        |
|      |        |
|      |        |
|      |        |
|      |        |
|      |        |
|      |        |
|      |        |
|      |        |

Apply the following settings:

- Page Orientation: Use the Paper Size tab displayed by the **File | Page Setup** command to change the page orientation to Landscape.

- Heading: Centre-align the heading, and make it Times New Roman, 20 point.

- Table: Create a two-column, 19-row table. Select the table and, using the Row tab displayed by the **Table | Table Properties** command, set the row height to 20 points.

Size
Rows 1-19:
☑ Specify height: 20 pt ⬍  Row height is: At least ▼

2 Choose **File | Save As**, and save the file as a template.

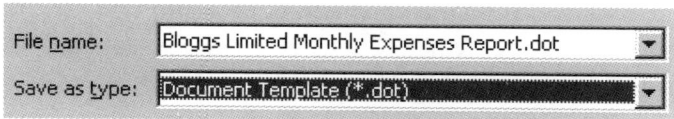

| File name: | Bloggs Limited Monthly Expenses Report.dot | ▼ |
|---|---|---|
| Save as type: | Document Template (*.dot) | ▼ |

3  Choose **File | Close** to close your new template.

4  Choose **File | New** to display the **General** tab of the New dialog box, where you can see your new template as an option. Select your new template and then click **OK**.

Word creates a new document based on your template. You can close the template.

# Styles and Outline view

Using styles in your Word documents offers another advantage: it allows you display documents in a way that reflects their structure. Such a structured view of a document is called an Outline view.

To switch to Outline view, choose **Views | Outline**. An Outline view of a document that is formatted using styles would typically look as follows:

 ⊕  **This·is·Heading·One·Style¶**
  ▫  This·is·body·text·(in·Normal)¶
   ⊕  **This·is·a·Heading·Two·Style¶**
    ▫  This·is·body·text·(in·Normal)¶
 ⊕  **This·is·Heading·One·Style¶**
  ▫  This·is·body·text·(in·Normal)¶

In the above example, three styles are applied: Heading 1, Heading 2, and Normal (the default, used for body text).

Notice that Word progressively indents styled text according to its level of importance in the document, starting with Heading 1.

To change from Outline view, choose the **View** menu and select the option **Normal** view or **Print Layout** view. These are explained in the next topic.

### Outline view

> *A view of a Word document that is formatted using styles. Outline view displays the structure of a document, with text indented progressively to reflect its level of importance.*

# Other document views

The two most common document views in Word are Normal and Print Layout.

## Normal view

Normal view is Word's default view for all new documents. It is the fastest view for typing, editing and scrolling. Any graphics or AutoShapes in the document are not displayed in this view. To switch to Normal view, choose **View | Normal.**

### Normal View

> *A view of a Word document that displays only text.*

## Print Layout view

If you insert a graphic or an AutoShape in a document, Word automatically switches to Print Layout view. While it is necessary for manipulating graphics and AutoShapes, Print Layout view may slow down such tasks as typing, editing, and scrolling. To switch to Print Layout view, choose **View | Print Layout.**

If you are working with a long document that contains a small number of graphics or AutoShapes, you may want to switch to Normal view.

### Print Layout view

*A view of a Word document that displays any graphics or AutoShapes in that document. It shows your document exactly as it will appear when you print it.*

You can close any open documents and exit Microsoft Word. You have now completed Chapter 5 of the ECDL *Word Processing* module.

# Chapter summary: so now you know

*Mail merge* is the process of combining a *form letter* (which holds the unchanging letter text) and a *data source* (which holds the names, addresses, and other details that are different in every merged letter).

The data source can be created in Word, or in a spreadsheet (such as Excel), or database (such as Access). Whichever the file type, the data source contents must be arranged in a table. Along the top row are the titles identifying the information categories in the columns underneath, such as Title or Last Name.

*Merge fields* in the form letter indicate which details are taken from the data source, and where they are positioned on the final, merged letter.

A *template* can act as a *document model* by storing built-in text and graphics such as your company's name and logo, preset formatting and text positioning, and preset page settings. A template can also act as an *interface controller* by specifying which of Word's menus, commands, and toolbars are available to the user.

A template, like a document, is a Word file. Whereas document file names end in .doc, template file names end in .dot.

Unless you choose otherwise, every new Word document you create is based on a template called *Normal.dot*. Word also provides templates for specific document types. You can create new templates, and change the template on which a document is based.

*Styles*, which are linked to templates, enable you to apply a bundle of formatting and text positioning settings to selected text in a single, quick operation.

In *Outline* view, you can display the structure of a document that has been formatted using styles. Use *Normal* view to display only the text in a document, and *Print Layout* view to display both text and any graphics or AutoShapes that it may contain.

## CHAPTER 6

# File formats and importing spreadsheet data

## In this chapter

In this chapter you will learn how Word 2000, as with all other applications, uses a particular file format. You will also discover how to convert your documents into other, non-Word 2000 file formats, so that they can be opened and read by people who work with applications other than Word 2000.

Copying and pasting within and between word documents was covered in previous chapters of this ECDL *Word Processing* module. This chapter takes you a step further, and shows you how to move data from a spreadsheet file to a word processor document. As you will see, you can transfer the data in either of two ways: pasting or embedding.

## New skills

At the end of this chapter you should be able to:
- Save Word 2000 documents in the following file formats: earlier versions of Word, RTF, WordPerfect, Text-Only, and HTML
- Explain the difference between pasting and embedding spreadsheet data in Word
- Paste spreadsheet data from Excel into a Word document
- Embed spreadsheet data from Excel into a Word document

## New words

At the end of this chapter you should be able to explain the following terms:
- File format

# File formats

I n Chapter 2, you met the term *format*, where it referred to items that affect the appearance of text in a Word document – italics, colours, bullets, and so on. When used alongside the word 'file', however, format has another, different meaning.

In ECDL Module 1, you learnt how all information stored on a computer consists ultimately of just two characters: 1 and 0. This raises two questions:

- When you open a file, how are these 1s and 0s translated into the text and graphics you see on your computer screen?

- And, when you save a file, how are the text and graphics converted back to 1s and 0s on your computer?

The answer is that the application developers apply a set of rules that translate between the 1s and 0s and the displayed text and graphics. Such a set of rules is called a file format.

### File format
*A set of rules that translates 1s and 0s into text and graphics on computer screens and printouts, and vice versa.*

A Word file, for example, is said to be in Word file format, an Excel file in Excel file format, and so on.

## Different applications, different file formats

Different software companies, however, use different rules for translating 1s and 0s into the text and graphics on screens and printouts.

Moreover, different versions of the one application often use different file formats. The Microsoft Word 2000 file format, for example, is different from the file format in some earlier versions of Word.

As you can imagine, these different file formats can create problems.

- In one company's file format, for example, the characters 10101010 might translate as the letter 'w' in Arial, 12-point italics, positioned 5 cm from the left page margin.

- In another, the same characters of 10101010 might convert to a thick blue line running down the left-hand side of the page.

## File name extensions

The format of a file is revealed by its three-letter file name extension, which the software application adds to the file name when the user saves the file.

The file name extension of .doc, for example, indicates a Word file, and .xls an Excel one. If you have worked with graphics files, you have probably met files with extensions such as .bmp, .gif, and .jpg.

The file format used in pages on the World Wide Web is HTML, which stands for HyperText Markup Language. HTML file names typically end in .htm.

# Word's file format options

Word 2000 offers you the ability to save your documents in a format other than its own. This feature is very useful when you want to give a file you have created to someone who uses a word processor other than Word 2000.

To view the file formats in which you can save your Word 2000 documents:

- Open a document.

- Choose **File | Save As**.

- Click on the arrow to the right of the Save as type: box.

| Save as type: | Word Document (*.doc) | ▼ |
|---|---|---|

| | |
|---|---|
| Word Document (*.doc) | ▲ |
| Web Page (*.htm; *.html) | |
| Document Template (*.dot) | |
| Rich Text Format (*.rtf) | |
| Text Only (*.txt) | |
| Text Only with Line Breaks (*.txt) | ▼ |

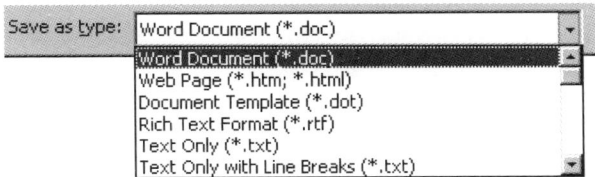

Only some of the listed options are relevant to this ECDL Word Processing Module.

### Previous Word versions

To save your Word 2000 document in an earlier Word file format, select either Word 6.0/95 or Word 2.x for Windows. Both file formats have the same file name extension as Word 2000 (.doc).

Saving a Word 2000 file in an earlier file format may result in some adjustment or loss of formatting.

### Rich text format

This is the common format of all Microsoft Office applications, including Word. A Word 2000 document saved in this file format looks just like one saved in Word 2000's own file format. The file name extension that is added is .rtf.

### WordPerfect format

Select from these options to save your document so that it can be opened and read within WordPerfect, another word processor application. Of the various WordPerfect options listed, the most commonly used is WordPerfect 5.x for Windows.

Converting a file from Word 2000 to WordPerfect may result in some adjustment or loss of formatting. The file name extension of WordPerfect for Windows files is also .doc.

### Text-only format

As its name suggests, this format saves only the text of a file. Any text formatting (such as bold or italics) or graphics contained in the Word 2000 file are lost. The file name extension added is .txt. This format is also called plain-text or ASCII format.

Only two of the various plain-text options offered by Word are relevant:

- **Text-Only**: Each paragraph of the original Word document occupies a single line of the plain-text file, often resulting in very long lines of text that you can view only by scrolling horizontally.

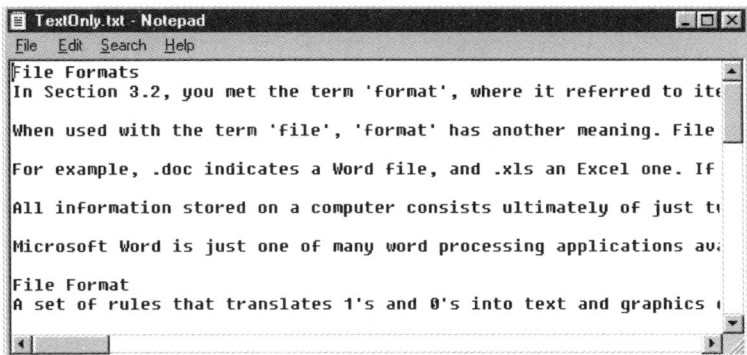

*A Text-Only file, viewed in Notepad*

- **Text-Only with Line Breaks**: A paragraph break is inserted everywhere a line ended in the original Word document, so that each line of the Word document becomes a separate paragraph in the plain-text file.

The advantage of this file format is that line width remains the same as in the original Word document, so that the text is easier to read on screen.

The disadvantage is that the plain-text file contains many more paragraph marks than the original Word file, and these can make editing the plain-text file awkward.

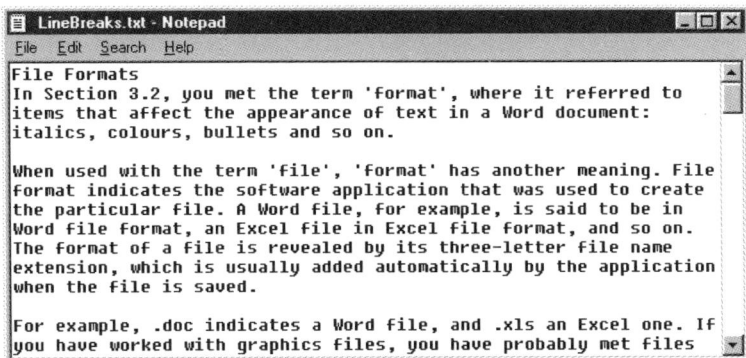

*A Text-Only with Line Breaks file, viewed in Notepad*

Because it is such a 'basic', no-frills format, plain-text files can be opened and read correctly by just about all software applications on virtually every type of computer. Plain-text is the file format most commonly used in electronic mail messages on the internet.

### HTML (web) format

Web pages are created using the HTML file format. The file name extension of this format is .htm (or, sometimes, .html).

You can save a Word 2000 file in HTML format in either of two ways:

- Choose **File | Save As Web Page**.

  –or–

- Choose **File | Save As**, and select the Save as Web Page (*.htm;*.html) option.

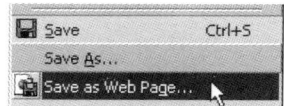

You can display and print HTML format files with a web browser application such as Microsoft Internet Explorer or Netscape Navigator.

# Embedding or pasting spreadsheet data

Microsoft Office applications (and most other Windows applications) allow you to transfer information between them. For this ECDL Module, you need only know how to insert data (text and numbers) into Word from the spreadsheet application, Microsoft Excel. In Excel, numbers and text are stored in little boxes called cells.

To transfer information from Excel to Word, follow these steps:

- Open the Excel file and select the required cells.

- Copy the selected Excel cells to the clipboard.

- Open the Word file and insert the Excel cells in Word.

## Pasting special options

The Word command you use for pasting Excel cells is **Edit | Paste Special**.

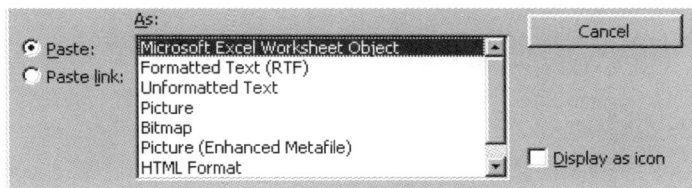

| | As: | | |
|---|---|---|---|
| ◉ Paste: | Microsoft Excel Worksheet Object | | Cancel |
| ○ Paste link: | Formatted Text (RTF) | | |
| | Unformatted Text | | |
| | Picture | | |
| | Bitmap | | ☐ Display as icon |
| | Picture (Enhanced Metafile) | | |
| | HTML Format | | |

The Paste Special dialog box offers the following options:

- **Paste** or **Paste link**: Leave this at the default of Paste.

- **Display as icon**: Leave this checkbox unselected.

- **As**: Two options are relevant here: Formatted Text (RTF) and Microsoft Excel Worksheet Object. These options are explained in the next two topics.

## Pasting from Excel

When you insert with the Formatted Text (RTF) option, the inserted spreadsheet data:

- Becomes fully part of Word

- Is displayed as a Word table

- Can be edited within Word itself

Pasting Excel data into Word in this way is similar to pasting from another Word document.

### Embedding from Excel

When you select with the Microsoft Excel Worksheet Object option, the inserted spreadsheet data:

- Is positioned within Word, but remains part of Excel

- Behaves like an imported graphic – it can be repositioned and resized by selecting and dragging

- Cannot be edited within Word.

If you try to edit the spreadsheet data in any way (to change a number, for example, or apply a different border style), Word's menu and toolbars disappear from your screen and are replaced by Excel's ones. Inserting data in this way brings with it the functionality of the application in which it was created. This is called *embedding*.

The following four exercises demonstrate pasting and embedding from Excel to Word.

In Exercise 6.1, you create two copies of an identical Word document. In Exercise 6.2, you create the Excel data for inserting into Word. In Exercises 6.3 and 6.4 you embed and paste your Excel data in the two Word documents.

## Exercise 6.1: Creating a Word document that you can embed and paste data into

1  Open Word and create a new document.

2  Type the following text and press Enter twice:

First Quarter Sales Figures

3  Select the text and make it Arial, Bold Italic, 22 point. Centre-align the text.

4  Type the following text and press Enter three times:

Congratulations everyone!

5  Select the text you typed in step 4 and make it Times New Roman, Italic, 24 point. Centre-align the text. Your document should now look as shown.

---

¶

## *First·Quarter·Sales·Figures¶*

*Congratulations·everyone!¶*

¶
¶

---

6  Save and name the Word document. If your initials are KB, for example, save it as KBsalesfigures1.doc.

7  Choose **File | Save As** to resave your Word document – but this time save it under a different name. For example, KBsalesfigures2.doc.

8  Choose **File | Open** and reopen the first saved version of your Word document.

You now have two Word documents, with identical content, open at the same time. You can switch between them using the Windows menu.

## Exercise 6.2: Creating an Excel data source file

1   Choose **Start | Programs | Microsoft Excel** to open a new Excel file on your screen.

2   Click on the cell at location C3, type the word January, and press Enter.

| | A | B | C | D | E |
|---|---|---|---|---|---|
| 1 | | | | | |
| 2 | | | | | |
| 3 | | | January | | |
| 4 | | | | | |
| 5 | | | | | |

3   Enter more text and numbers to Excel as shown below.

| | A | B | C | D | E |
|---|---|---|---|---|---|
| 1 | | | | | |
| 2 | | | | | |
| 3 | | | January | February | March |
| 4 | | Product 1 | 213 | 345 | 698 |
| 5 | | Product 2 | 180 | 245 | 401 |
| 6 | | Product 3 | 270 | 389 | 528 |
| 7 | | Product 4 | 134 | 262 | 390 |
| 8 | | Product 5 | 90 | 154 | 310 |

4   When finished, save the Excel file. If your initials are KB, for example, save it as KBsalesfigures.xls. Leave the Excel file open on your screen.

5   Click on cell B3 and hold down the mouse button. Drag rightwards and down to cell E8.

| | A | B | C | D | E |
|---|---|---|---|---|---|
| 1 | | | | | |
| 2 | | | | | |
| 3 | | | January | February | March |
| 4 | | Product 1 | 213 | 345 | 698 |
| 5 | | Product 2 | 180 | 245 | 401 |
| 6 | | Product 3 | 270 | 389 | 528 |
| 7 | | Product 4 | 134 | 262 | 390 |
| 8 | | Product 5 | 90 | 154 | 310 |
| 9 | | | | | |
| 10 | | | | | |

6  Choose **Edit | Copy** to copy the selected Excel cells to the clipboard.

You may now close the Excel file, but, for Exercise 6.3 to work, you must not exit the Excel application.

## Exercise 6.3: Embedding the Excel data in Word

1  Use the **Window | <document name>** command to display the first Word document that you saved (in this example, KBsalesfigures1.doc), and then click the last paragraph mark in that document.

2  Choose **Edit | Paste Special**, select the Microsoft Excel Worksheet Object option, and click **OK**.

The option is available only when the Excel application is open on your computer.)

This embeds the Excel data from the clipboard to the Word document.

3  Click on the bottom-right handle of the inserted data, and drag it until the inserted data is centred between the left and right page margins. Your Word document should now look like that shown.

*First·Quarter·Sales·Figures¶*

*Congratulations·everyone!¶*

|          | January | February | March |
|----------|---------|----------|-------|
| Product 1 | 213 | 345 | 698 |
| Product 2 | 180 | 245 | 401 |
| Product 3 | 270 | 389 | 528 |
| Product 4 | 134 | 262 | 390 |
| Product 5 | 90 | 145 | 310 |

You can work with the embedded data area just as you can with a graphic: you select it and reposition and resize it. You cannot edit it, however, at least not in Word.

To change the embedded data in any way – edit a number, delete a row, or add a coloured border – you must first double-click on it. This action causes Word's menus and toolbars to be replaced by Excel ones. Try it and see. Your screen should look as shown.

**First·Quarter·Sales·Figures¶**

*Congratulations·everyone!¶*

|   | B | C | D | E |
|---|---|---|---|---|
| 3 |   | January | February | March |
| 4 | Product 1 | 213 | 345 | 698 |
| 5 | Product 2 | 180 | 245 | 401 |
| 6 | Product 3 | 270 | 389 | 528 |
| 7 | Product 4 | 134 | 262 | 390 |
| 8 | Product 5 | 90 | 145 | 310 |

Sheet1 / Sheet2 / Sheet3 /

To return to Word, click anywhere on the Word document, outside the embedded spreadsheet area. Save your Word document.

You can now exit Excel. You do not need it open for Exercise 6.4.

### Exercise 6.4: Pasting the Excel data in Word

1  Use the **Window | <document Name>** command to display the second Word document that you saved (in this example, KBsalesfigures2.doc), and then click the last paragraph mark in that document.

2  Choose **Edit | Paste Special**, select the Formatted Text (RTF) option, and click **OK**.

(The option is available whether Excel is open or not.)

This pastes the Excel data from the clipboard to the Word document. The spreadsheet cells have the format of a Word table.

3 Click anywhere in the table, choose **Table | Table AutoFormat**, select the Classic 2 option, and click **OK**.

4 Drag the vertical edges of the column borders until the table is centred evenly between the left and right margins of the page.

5 With the cursor anywhere in the table, choose **Table | Select | Table**. On the Formatting toolbar, change the font size to 14 point.

Your Word document should now look like that shown.

### *First·Quarter·Sales·Figures¶*

¶

*Congratulations·everyone!¶*

¶

| | January¤ | February¤ | March¤ |
|---|---|---|---|
| **Product·1¤** | 213 | 345 | 698 |
| **Product·2¤** | 180 | 245 | 401 |
| **Product·3¤** | 270 | 389 | 528 |
| **Product·4¤** | 134 | 262 | 390 |
| **Product·5¤** | 90 | 145 | 310 |

6 Save your Word document. You have finished the embedding and pasting exercises, and you can close both Word documents.

You have now completed the final chapter of the ECDL *Word Processing* module. Congratulations.

# Chapter summary: so now you know

A *file format* is a set of rules that translates between the 1s and 0s used by the computer to store information and the text and graphics displayed on screens and on printouts. Different applications – even different versions of the same application – can use different and incompatible file formats.

To help you share your files with others, Word 2000 allows you save your documents in a file format other than its own. The options include: earlier versions of Microsoft Word, RTF (the common Microsoft Office file format), WordPerfect (another word processor), and HTML (the Web page file format).

You can also save a Word document as a *text-only* file, so that it can be opened and read by virtually all applications on all types of computers. Any formatting or graphics in the Word document are lost, however.

You can insert spreadsheet data from Excel to Word in either of two ways: pasting or embedding.

*Pasted data* becomes part of the Word document: it is displayed as a Word table, and can be edited within Word itself. Inserting Excel data into Word in this way is similar to pasting from another Word document.

*Embedded* spreadsheet data, while positioned within the Word document, remains part of Excel; it behaves like an imported graphic and cannot be edited within Word. If you try to edit the spreadsheet data in any way, Word's menu and toolbars are replaced on screen by Excel's ones. Embedded data brings with it the functionality of the application in which it was created.

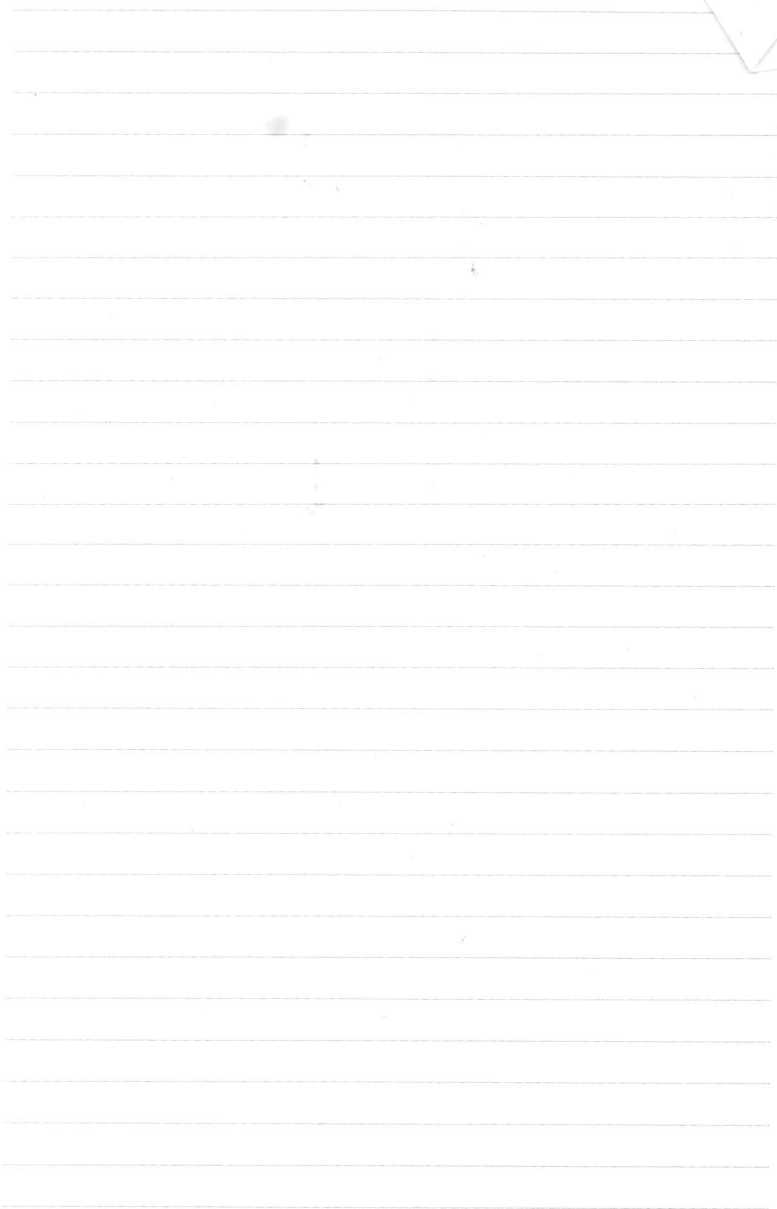